LUCKNOW CHRONICLES

Memories, Musings, Myths

LUCKNOW CHRONICLES

Memories, Musings, Myths

PC Sarkar

KALPAZ

Published by

Kalpaz Publications
C-30, Satyawati Nagar,
Delhi – 110052
Ph.: 011-47034999, 9811692060
www.kalpazpublications.com
E-mail: kalpaz@hotmail.com

Distribution Network
www.gyanbooks.com
India, USA, Canada, UK, Australia, France

ISBN: 978-93-5722-346-1
First Published, 2023

Printed at: Gyan Press, Delhi.

LUCKNOW CHRONICLES
Memories, Musings, Myths
Author: PC SARKAR

This book is dedicated to the city of Lucknow and to all the good that it still stands for...

- PC Sarkar

"A concerted effort to preserve our heritage is a vital link to our cultural, educational, aesthetic, inspirational and economic legacies - all of the things that quite literally make us who we are"

- Steve Berry

"To know nothing of what happened before you, is to forever remain a child"

- Cicero

CONTENTS

LIST OF FIGURES

Chapter VI

Chapter - I

A Question of Inheritance

Historical Background

The *Nawabi* (later *Badshahi*) dynasty of Awadh commenced with the appointment of Mir Mohammad Amin of Nishapur or Neyshabur (Iran) as *Subadar* (provincial Governor) of Awadh *suba* (province) on September 9, 1722, by the Mughal Emperor, Mohammad Shah "Rangila." Earlier, the former had been honoured with the title of Sa'adat Khan Bahadur Burhan-ul-Mulk Bahadur Jang by the Mughal court, but he would be known in history simply as Burhan-ul-Mulk. He had five daughters (his only son having died of small pox during childhood) and so he gave his eldest daughter, Sadr un-Nisan or Sadr-i-Jahan's hand in marriage to his nephew, Muhammad Mirza Muqim, the son of his eldest sister. Sadr-i-Jahan herself was purported to be the daughter of a slave girl, attached to Burhan-ul-Mulk's wife. The succession pattern in the *Nawabi* / *Badshahi* regime of Lucknow (1722 - 1856) thus commenced on a sticky wicket.

The *Nawabi* and *Wizarat* Phase

As in other medieval regimes, the question of inheritance and succession continued to doggedly follow Awadh's rulers. The reasons for this were manifold - the first and foremost being the absence of the principle of *primogeniture* (first born legitimate child to inherit the ruler's entire or main estate), or more specifically, *agnatic primogeniture* (inheritance of the first born son) and *matrilineal primogeniture* (inheritance by the first born daughter). So it was not mandatory for the first born child to succeed his father on the *masnad* (royal seat), later throne. In any case, the designation of *Subadar* or *Nawab* (derived from *Naib*, or deputy) or *Wazir* (Prime Minister) were not hereditary, either in the Mughal court or in the courts of Faizabad / Lucknow, as will be detailed later. Another issue that frequently arose was the question of legitimacy. Historians and writers have mentioned that some of the successor nominees or appointees were not quite legitimate or of noble blood, and might have been introduced in the court surreptitiously, by unethical means, to serve a purpose. The Nawabi court was rife with politics, including *zenana* (female quarters) politics, and cases where the ruler himself first declared someone as his son and successor, and then repudiated him, were also not rare. To this chaos, a fourth angle was introduced, when the British anointed Ghazi-ud-Din Haider as an independent king (*Badshah*) in 1818, but each of his successors had to be approved and appointed by the Company (together with a new Treaty or set of demands). The fifth and last aspect of this baffling situation, involving Nawabi succession was the "unsuitability" of the successor himself. But who was to judge this unsuitability? That remained the moot question. In the following pages, we shall discuss, with specific examples, the issues of inheritance in the Awadh court, which cropped up during almost each succession.

Burhan-ul-Mulk was never honoured by the *Wizarat* of the Mughal court. His son-in-law and nominated successor, Muhammad Muqim, honoured by the title of Abul-Mansur Khan Safdarjang or Safdar Jang was Nawab of Awadh from March 10, 1739 to October 26, 1754. He held the *Wizarat* of Delhi from April 28, 1748 till May 13, 1753. Safdar Jang had been earlier nominated as *Naib* of Burhan-ul-Mulk in Awadh (1724 - 1739), the tenure proving invaluable for gaining administrative experience, both civil and military. However, despite his nomination, his actual accession to the post of Nawab of Awadh was not so easy. A close contender was Sher Jang, his cousin brother. Both cousins petitioned Nadir Shah, pleading for the post. Sher Jang was the son of Siyadat Khan, Burhan-ul-Mulk's elder brother, whereas Safdar Jang was the son of Burhan-ul-Mulk's sister. A petition was submitted before the Emperor, stating that neither Sher Jang nor Safdar Jang were in the direct line of succession to Burhan-ul-Mulk; that the post was anyhow not hereditary, and depended entirely on the Mughal emperor's pleasure and preference. But if any one of the two contenders was to be considered, then Safdar Jang should be preferred since he had been nominated by Burhan-ul-Mulk. Also, Safdar Jang had acquired ample administrative and military experience as *Naib* of Burhan-ul-Mulk in Awadh.

A third more practical angle to this succession was the financial capacities of the contenders; Safdar Jang had access to the treasury at Faizabad, and the wily Nadir Shah recommended his candidature to the Mughal Emperor, after accepting two crores of rupees, costly gifts and presents, obtained from Faizabad and Burhan-ul-Mulk's house in Delhi. After Nadir Shah's departure, Emperor Mohammad Shah conferred all the titles and honours and *jagirs* due to Safdar Jang as successor to Burhan-ul-Mulk. A murky chapter had come to an end.

Jalal-ud-Din Haider was born on January 19, 1732, being the only child of Safdar Jang and the accomplished Sadr un-Nisan or Nawab Begum. His maternal grandfather, Burhan-ul-Mulk doted on him, looking upon him as his future heir. He was barely eight years old when his grandfather died and his father became Nawab of Awadh. By the age of twelve, he had free access to the Mughal court, his father now being the *Wazir* at Delhi. It was Mohammad Shah who arranged his *nikah* (arranged marriage) with Amat ul-Zohra (later known as Bahu Begum), the daughter of Ishaq Khan Mohammad Moatm-ud-Daula, a much favoured nobleman in the Mughal court. In actuality, Mohammad Shah wanted to unite the families of Safdar Jang and Ishaq Khan through this alliance. The marriage was a lavish affair by all accounts, the groom being fourteen years old and the bride younger by a year or two. July 16, 1748 saw the title of Shuja-ud-Daula Bahadur being conferred on the young man and him being appointed as *Mir Atish* (Head of artillery). Shuja-ud-Daula was merely sixteen years old then. On August 3, 1750, Shuja-ud-Daula was appointed as the *Naib Wazir* in the Mughal court, due to the absence of his father from Delhi. But things began to go downhill from this point onwards.

By the end of September, 1750, a rumour was spread about the death and defeat of Safdar Jang in one of his campaigns in the south, and the noblemen who had been inimical towards the Nawab Wazir started plotting not only against Safdar Jang (who was very much alive), but also against his son, Shuja, with a view of overthrowing both father and son and confiscating their properties at Delhi. The vacillating nature of Ahmad Shah, the Mughal Emperor did not stabilise the situation. On the advice of his mother, Shuja boldly held on to his post, till Safdar Jang returned. But the spark of revolt had been lit, the prime conspirator being Javed Khan, an eunuch, who had considerable influence over Ahmad Shah. Safdar Jang, on his return, had the eunuch stabbed to death on September 6, 1752. However, the relief obtained from the removal of Javed Khan was short-lived. Safdar Jang re-assumed full powers as *Wazir* and redistributed the various offices and posts, giving his son, Shuja, the maximum benefit of this exercise. Quite understandably, this did not go down well with the other nobles in the court; the queen mother, who had been close to the late Javed Khan, swore retribution. The Emperor was also feeling stifled with the *Wazir's* conduct, paving the way for Safdar Jang's dismissal. On March 17, 1753, Safdar Jang, his family and retainers were thrown out of the Red Fort, guns being trained towards the *Wazir's* house. The infuriated *Wazir* left with his son, preparing to do battle and regain his honour.

May 5, 1753 saw Shuja being removed from all his official obligations, including the command of the Imperial artillery (*Mir Atish*). When Safdar Jang retaliated by plundering *Shahjahanabad*, the infuriated Emperor formally dismissed the *Wazir* from his post on May 13, 1753. This mutinous situation between the Emperor and his ex-*Wazir* continued for six months, after which peace was negotiated between the two warring parties. Safdar Jang and Shuja left for Lucknow on November 7, 1753. Safdar Jang died an untimely death on October 5, 1754, throwing open the question of his successor as Nawab of Awadh. Till this point of time, Shuja had not exhibited any significant leadership qualities, although to be fair, he was only 22 years of age, at the time of Safdar Jang's demise. His (and his father's) rivals had succeeded in removing Safdar Jang and his family from Delhi. The future looked bleak for the young man, although he was firmly ensconced in Awadh. But fate proved to be favourable once again.

Ahmad Shah soon fell out with his protégé, Imad-ul-Mulk (the main rival of Safdar Jang and Shuja, who had been instrumental in throwing out Safdar Jang from the Mughal court). The current *Wazir*, Intizam-ud-Daula, was also alarmed at Imad-ul-Mulk's successes, the latter by now had emerged as the new regent, due to his alliance with the Marathas. In a skirmish between the forces of Ahmad Shah and Imad-ul-Mulk, the former was defeated (popularly known as the *Sikandarabad Incident*) and forced to flee, with the queen mother. Ahmad Shah was apprehended, imprisoned and blinded. Alamgir II was propped up as the successor of Ahmad Shah, but the relationship between him and Imad-ul-Mulk soon deteriorated, due to the latter's high-handed ways. On October 11, 1754, Alamgir II appointed Shuja as the successor of Safdar Jang. However, the *Wizarat* of Delhi still eluded Shuja, and the title was conferred to him on December 24, 1759, only after the assassination of Alamgir II in November 1759.

Shuja's rule in Awadh and his *Wizarat* at Delhi were highly eventful, but it is beyond the scope of this book Chapter to discuss his successes and failures. Shuja died on January 26, 1775. Writers have expressed the view that he was not in favour of Asaf-ud-Daula (Mirza Amani) succeeding him, but preferred the candidature of Sa'adat Ali Khan* (Mirza Mangli). Apparently, Nawab Begum (mother of the late Shuja) had also advised Bahu Begum thus, "Your son, Asaf-ud-Daula, is now twenty six years old, but till now, although being the eldest son of Shuja, he has devoted his time in activities which do not suit his stature. He does not have the necessary capability of handling administrative duties. It is likely that the riches that your husband has accumulated would be frittered way in a short period. Mirza Sa'adat Ali is more intelligent and capable. I would advise you to keep Asaf as a nominal Nawab, with Sa'adat Ali as Minister." This did not go down well with the proud Bahu Begum, who snapped, "I have but one son, good or bad, whatever he might be. In your eyes, all sons of Shuja are equal!" To this, Nawab Begum replied, "I have merely expressed my opinion. You can do whatever pleases you, but you will be solely responsible for the consequences of your actions." Both *begums* seemed to disregard the fact that the post of Nawab was not hereditary, and had to be ratified by the Mughal court. But as history

---

* Erroneously referred to as Sa'adat Ali Khan II in some sources.

would show, Asaf assumed the post of *Nawab* on January 27, 1775. He had to wait for more than a year, to be appointed as *Wazir* in April, 1776. By this time, with the weakening of the Mughal Emperor, increasing British influence, coupled with Maratha depredations, the significance of the *Wazir's* post had diminished considerably. Asaf-ud-Daula remained content with his own interests and way of life, controversial as they might have been. He was not a warrior like his illustrious father, nor did he ever visit the Mughal court at Delhi. All through his lifetime, Asaf remained apprehensive of Sa'adat Ali Khan's motives, actions and apparent popularity, as well as the latter's continued hobnobbing with the British. On his part, Sa'adat Ali did nothing to assuage the fears of Asaf. Indeed, Sa'adat Ali remained a maverick in his youth, till such time he was finally appointed as Nawab, which we shall discuss a little later in this Chapter.

Asaf-ud-Daula died on September 21, 1797. Writers are unanimous to state that he had not led a normal conjugal life with his wife, Shams un-Nisan or Dulhan Begum; that the marriage had never been consummated (discussed in another Chapter). Indeed, some historians have branded Asaf as a homosexual. Contrary to this, it is also true that the Nawab had a sizeable harem, with "500 of the greatest beauties (Qureshi, 2003)." They enjoyed *jagirs*, perquisites and monetary stipends during his lifetime but almost starved to death after him. So how did a homosexual ruler enjoy the pleasures of an extensive harem, consisting of female beauties? This question remains unanswered. Despite his sexual predilections, Asaf did not have an heir from his chief consort, Shams un-Nisan. An interesting narrative had been given by Basu (1943) regarding Asaf's successor, including the various political manoeuvres and undercurrents that ultimately paved the way for Wazir Ali becoming the Nawab of Awadh (albeit for a very short term), on the very same day, i.e. on September 21, 1797, duly recognised by Bahu Begum and the nobility of Awadh. Wazir Ali's parentage remained shrouded in mystery. He could have been Asaf's offspring, from a (menial) woman not married to him; another theory afloat was that Wazir Ali was the son of a *farrash* (menial servant, cleaning floors, carpets etc.), whose wife had been introduced in Asaf's *zenana*, when she was already pregnant.

Asaf-ud-Daula had notified the Calcutta government about the "birth" of three children, in March 1779, and in May and September

1780. All these children died subsequently and their deaths were also notified. Wazir Ali's "birth" went un-notified, and yet Asaf had presented Wazir as his son and heir to Bristow, the British Resident stationed in Lucknow. In 1794, Wazir Ali's marriage was celebrated by pomp and show in thc *Aishbagh* gardens of Lucknow and he was subsequently appointed as *Diwan* (revenue collector) in 1796. Three days after the death of Asaf, Mirza Jangli and other sons of Shuja-ud-Daula residing at Lucknow informed John Lumsden (British Resident at Lucknow, 1793 - 1799) that although they did not dispute Wazir Ali's succession, they would not be able to pay the customary *nazars* (ceremonial gifts presented in court to royalty / nobility), or show the "outer marks of respect" due to Wazir Ali's low origin. October 4, 1797 saw Mirza Mangli or Sa'adat Ali claiming the *masnad* at Lucknow, by virtue of the eldest surviving member of the line of Safdar Jang and Wazir Ali having no relationship with Asaf-ud-Daula. On October 17, Sa'adat Ali wrote another letter to John Shore, then Governor General at Calcutta, offering to fulfil all the earlier engagements between Asaf-ud-Daula and the EIC, provided the latter helped him to ascend the *masnad.* It needs to be noted here that no one approached the Mughal court for ratification of the Nawab's appointment.

Despite the various pressures building upon him, Shore decided to go ahead with Wazir Ali's anointment, because the case against Wazir Ali was based on heresy. Not one claimant or dissenter had been able to offer documentary proof regarding Wazir Ali's purported illegitimacy. The latter also had the support of the venerable Bahu Begum. Also, it seems that Sa'adat Ali was not quite welcome by the Nawabi court of Lucknow, because he was an Anglophile. But if Wazir Ali did have dubious origins, why did Bahu Begum support him? Possibly she might have desired to be on the British side, who, till now, had not displayed an iota of interest in Sa'adat Ali's candidature, and the latter, in any case, had been opposed by her, even during the appointment of Asaf-ud-Daula. The *begum* might have envisioned Wazir Ali as a puppet governor, so she could wield the true power in Awadh politics. Wazir Ali was perceived to be very youthful and docile, hence malleable, both by the British and Bahu Begum. Anyway, whatever might have been the reason for Wazir Ali's success, subsequent events would prove that both

Bahu Begum and the British had miscalculated. Wazir Ali was a simmering inferno, biding his time.

By the time Shore reached Lucknow on December 23, the political scenario had changed considerably. Wazir Ali had grown suspicious of British intentions and had started amassing an army. He had applied for the title of *Wazir* from the Mughal emperor, but it was yet to be ratified. Shore increased his own security, carried out surreptitious investigations for a month and by January 1798, "concluded" that none of the so-called sons of Asaf-ud-Daula were actually born of him, and that the line of succession should revert to that of Shuja-ud-Daula. This would entail the removal of Wazir Ali and the elevation of Sa'adat Ali to the *masnad.* It was observed that the young Nawab, since his accession, had "exhibited a series of actions - mean, profligate and vicious." That he showed signs of "levity and insensibility, even viciousness." A perfect case of giving an (under)dog a bad name and hanging him. True to her nature, Bahu Begum now offered Shore an additional 20 lakh rupees annually in subsidy, if he raised Azad-ud-Daula (Mirza Jangli), Shuja's third son, to the *masnad.* Indeed, Bahu Begum was prepared to go to any lengths to prevent Sa'adat Ali's candidature for the *masnad*; her propensity to play power politics was boundless, her aversion for Sa'adat Ali was visceral.

Despite all these manoeuvres and counter-manoeuvres, fate had to ultimately come to a full circle. The British, who had fought a bitter war in 1764 against Shuja at Buxar, were now eager to promote the continuity of his lineage, ostensibly to serve the Company's political interests in Awadh. For this purpose, they found Sa'adat Ali to be most suitable, although they had shown no interest in him, for the past two decades. On February 21, 1798, a treaty was signed between Sa'adat Ali and the Company. From the roof of *Bibiapur Kothi* in Lucknow, Wazir Ali saw his uncle, in full regalia, accompanied by John Shore, approaching the city to take up his new assignment. Wazir Ali would be shortly involved in the murder of George Cherry, former Resident of Lucknow. He would raise the banner of revolt against the British, be captured and imprisoned at Fort William in Calcutta. Awadh's stormy succession politics would, however, continue.

Sa'adat Ali was the second son of Shuja-ud-Daula. With all the discussion on Wazir Ali's parentage above, Sa'adat Ali's origins were also not spotless or unambiguous. His mother's name is not available on record. Writers surmise that she was a *khurd* (junior) *begum* of Shuja, a *mut'ah* wife. Other writers with more fanciful imaginations have averred that she was actually a Rajput princess, whose real name was Rani Chattar Kunwar and the *Chattar Manzil* palace in Lucknow was built in her honour, by her grandson, Ghazi-ud-Din Haider. Since she had given birth to a son, she acquired the status of *mahal,* as per tradition of the Nawabi court. Whatever might have been the antecedents of Sa'adat Ali's biological mother, she never got any importance as long as Shuja was alive. Bahu Begum did not let the junior *begums* speak or even sit in her presence. All this rankled Sa'adat Ali, who felt that his mother was not getting the regard due to her. When Sa'adat Ali became Nawab, he invited his mother to stay with him at Lucknow. Almost adjacent to the *Rumi Darwaza*, the *Sunheri Burj* or *Burj Teela* palace was situated (which is no longer extant), where Bahu Begum used to reside whenever she visited Lucknow (Fig. 17). Sa'adat's mother took to riding with full pomp and show alongside the Gomti river, and her cavalcade would pass in front of Bahu Begum's palace, with the beating of drums and sounding of trumpets. Understandably, this caused annoyance to the haughty Bahu Begum and she forbade the retinue to pass by her residence.

Sa'adat Ali's nameless mother, referred to respectfully as *Janab-e-Alia*, a generalised title, is also credited for initiating the *Bada Mangal* festival and building of the old Mahabir temple in Aliganj, Lucknow, died in September, 1808 at the age of 70 years. She was interred in an octagonal mausoleum, which is extant today (although in ruins and heavily encroached) which is popularly known as *Janab-e-Alia* tomb in Golaganj area of old Lucknow. It is an elegant structure in its own right, but nowhere near to Bahu Begum's tomb in magnificence (*Bahu Begum ka Maqbara*) at Faizabad.

Sa'adat Ali Khan, as we have noted, was ambitious and devious, but he lacked that murderous and ruthless instinct which could have made him Nawab much earlier, after the death of his father. He kept Asaf on tenterhooks all through his life, but never made any armed attempt to capture Asaf's seat or undermine his authority; indeed, he seemed to prefer a wait-and-watch policy, which would last for more than two decades, before he could occupy what was perhaps rightfully due to him. Once, in an armed attack on Asaf's camp by disgruntled courtiers, ostensibly egged on by Sa'adat Ali himself, the latter, armed with sword and gun, came face to face with Asaf, who was unarmed and to his credit, unafraid. But instead of taking advantage of the situation, Sa'adat chose to retreat. Sa'adat was 50 years of age when he finally became Nawab. He is recognised for being an efficient, parsimonious administrator and a prolific builder. But the wait for his inheritance cost him the best years of his life. He was mentioned as *Wazir* by the Mughal emperor, without the investiture actually taking place.

Sa'adat Ali Khan's first wife (*Khas Mahal*) was Afzal un-Nisan Begum, who died in Benaras in June 7, 1826. When Sa'adat Ali died on July 10, 1814, he was succeeded by Ghazi-ud-Din Haider, the son of Begum Khurshid Zadi, his second wife. Ghazi-ud-Din's inheritance was clear, but he was to create a different kind of controversy as we shall see later on. In fact, weary of British pressures, Sa'adat Ali had once even wished to abdicate in favour of Ghazi-ud-Din Haider, indicating that the latter was the choice as successor of the ruling Nawab. The tombs of both Sa'adat Ali and Khurshid Zadi, built by their son, Ghazi-ud-Din Haider, are extant in Lucknow and are magnificent structures, wholly based on the principles of Islamic architecture.

Sa'adat Ali Khan had ten sons and five daughters. His second son was Shams-ud-Daula who, as per tradition, held the rank of *Jarnail* (Commander / General of the armed forces), having five sons and two daughters. Iqbal-ud-Daula, the second son of Shams-ud-Daula fancied himself as the true successor to the Nawabi *masnad*. We shall discuss his actions a little later in this Chapter.

The *Badshahi* Phase

Ghazi-ud-Din Haider secured the title of *Wazir* from the Mughal Emperor during the commencement of his Nawabi tenure. He remained as Nawab Wazir from July 10, 1814 to October 8, 1819. It has been alluded that during his father's lifetime, he had been deliberately kept in the background, and not allowed to take part in public affairs; that he had not even been permitted to learn English. But this does not ring true, taking into account Sa'adat Ali's desire (see above) to abdicate in his favour. In 1819, the British came across a puerile idea to elevate Ghazi-ud-Din to the status of an independent monarch, thereby severing the century old relationship between the Mughal empire and Awadh. He was encouraged to wear an European-style "crown", sit on a throne (instead of seat) and mint coins in his own name. Edward Paget, the British Commander-in-Chief in India, observed that he was "an extremely good and kind hearted man, but like myself, preferring anything and everything to his business. Accordingly, instead of attending to affairs of State, he spends his time in boat-building and house-building, in turning, in printing, in collecting European and especially English commodities of all sorts, descriptions and kinds, and, in short, idling." Ghazi-ud-Din remained a titular king from 1819 onwards; he died at the *Farhat Baksh* Palace, Lucknow, on October 19, 1827 and was buried in *Shahnajaf,* the mausoleum he had built for himself.

Although Ghazi-ud-Din had a sizeable harem, his chief consort, Badshah Begum, could not give him a male heir to the throne. Even during his lifetime, there was a scandalous controversy regarding his future successor and heir to the throne. The first king of Awadh had two more senior queens, Mubarak Mahal and Sultan Mariam Begum, both having European blood. Mubarak Mahal was the daughter of Col. Aish of Cawnpore. Mariam Begum was originally Mary Short, who converted to Islam on her marriage but reverted as a Roman Catholic when widowed; she was the elder daughter of Dr. James Short, a Roman Catholic in the service of the Company, by his wife, Mary Minas, an Armenian lady. But we are digressing. Ironically, it was a maidservant, Subh Daulat, who had been elevated as the fourth *begum* of Ghazi-ud-Din Haider, with the title of Nawab Mumtaz Mahal, whose son became the second king of Awadh. In *Tarikh Badshah Begam* (1938), the biographical account of Badshah Begum, it is specifically mentioned that not long after his marriage with Badshah Begum, Ghazi-ud-Din Haider was attracted to Subh Daulat, a maidservant attached to his wife. The latter became pregnant, and after the child was born, the mother of the new-born child was killed with "unsurpassable cruelty" at the instigation of the furious Badshah

Begum. The *begum* was wont to kill the child also, but was prevented from committing the unspeakable horror by her own courtiers. The child was to become Nasir-ud-Din Haider, the second king of Awadh, under the tutelage of Badshah Begum herself. However, Nasir-ud-Din's antecedents were not above doubt. When the young king's relations became estranged with Badshah Begum, the latter was supposed to have written to the British, stating that Nasir-ud-Din was not the real son of the late Ghazi-ud-Din Haider, but the offspring of a *dhobi* (washer man). In the initial stages of his rule. Nasir-ud-Din remained apprehensive over Badshah Begum's clout in the royal court and remained subservient to his adoptive mother's wishes; he remembered that earlier, Bahu Begum at Faizabad had first advocated the ascendancy of Wazir Ali and then had withdrawn her support, and he did want to create a similar situation for himself (Sleeman, 1858). But fate had other plans.

Nasir-ud-Din's mother, Subh Daulat, had been murdered (September 9, 1803) at the instigation of Badshah Begum, already discussed above. On ascending the throne (October 19, 1827), one of the first actions of Nasir-ud-Din, was the construction of a mausoleum over the remains of his mother at *Jhankar Bagh*, where she had been hurriedly buried in a graveyard meant for the poor. The tomb is extant today, but in a ruinous, dilapidated condition. Nasir-ud-Din was married to Ruqaiya Sultan Begum, a Mughal princess, who preferred to stay away from her husband, due to his frivolities and amorous nature. This chaotic state of affairs in his harem would ultimately lead to his untimely death, with the question of his succession looming up once again.

One of the numerous wives of Nasir-ud-Din was Sharaf un-Nisan or Afzal Mahal, a former slave girl, called Sukh Chain, whom he had married in 1817. Her son, Faridun Bakht, more popularly known as Munna Jaan, was born at Lucknow on September 14, 1820. This "birth" set off a perplexing chain of events in the Nawabi court which remain unsolved to this day. It might be noted that Nasir-ud-Din Haider was a prince and successor designate to Ghazi-ud-Din Haider during the "birth" of Munna Jaan. However, the king refused to acknowledge his grandson, stating that the child was the offspring of a washer woman, who had been surreptitiously introduced into the *zenana* by Badshah Begum, about 25 days before the infant was born. Sukh Chain herself had been married to the young prince on the orders of Badshah Begum. Later, a letter purported to have been written under Badshah Begum's seal stated that Sukh Chain had been pregnant for 27 months and could deliver the child only after the necessary rituals had been followed and the evil influences on the mother had been exorcised. The letter further stated that Sukh Chain was again pregnant for four years. The then Resident, Mordant Ricketts attempted to send the Residency Surgeon and other officials to examine the lady who had been pregnant for four years, but they were denied access.

We shall now go back a little in time to discuss another piece of this jig-saw puzzle which had been introduced with the entry of a Dulari as wet nurse for Munna Jaan soon after his birth. So who was this Dulari, who would later be given the title of honorific title of Mallika Zamani and she would wield considerable clout in the court of Nasir-ud-Din Haider (albeit for a short while)? A discussion on her antecedents, according to different versions, obtained under oath, would cover quite a few pages, so we shall try to be brief:

Version 1: Dulari was a Hindu, a *kurmi* (tiller) by caste who had been pawned by her mother to one Talat Murad, in lieu of the money due to him. Talat Murad's illegitimate son, Rustom married her and they had a son named Mohammad Ali. After the death of Talat, Rustom and his family faced deprivation, as a result of which, Rustom left Lucknow taking up the job of a syce (groomer of horses), while his estranged wife worked as a wet nurse in different families. By now Mohammad Ali was three years old and Dulari had a infant daughter, when Munna Jaan was born in the palace and Dulari was selected to become his wet nurse, from among a number of candidates.

Version 2: A slave girl, Hussaini was in the service of a Hulum (*sic*) un-Nisan, having being procured from one Bolur (*sic*) Khan, a foot soldier, for 30 rupees. On the death of Hulum (*sic*) un-Nisan, Hussaini became the property of Gauhar un-Nisan, the daughter of the deceased Hulum (*sic*). The son of Hulum got employment in Benaras and invited his sister, Gauhar, to join him. The latter was penniless, so she pawned Hussaini with one Rustom, an elephant coolie; the latter promptly seduced the female slave and made her pregnant. Ashamed of his actions, Rustom sought permission from his mistress, Gauhar and subsequently married Hussaini. A son, Mohammad was born of this union. Hussaini took service as a wet nurse with several families, after she gave birth to a daughter. This continued till she was appointed as a wet nurse in the royal household, described above.

Version 3: Sheikh Talib Murad, whose family was originally from Shahjahanabad had a sister named Karamat un-Nisan. A person from the *kurmi* tribe (see above) borrowed a sum of 60 rupees from Karamat, and being unable to repay the loan, gave her daughter, Dulari, in lieu of repayment of the debt. Karamat adopted this girl as her own daughter and called her Hussaini, who proved to be of "loose and abandoned character." Her mistress, Karamat, therefore removed Hussaini's privileges and kept her as a slave. Around this time, a widow arrived in the city, accompanied by her son, Rustom. Sheikh Talib Murad took her as his second wife, but Rustom developed an illegitimate relationship with the slave girl, Hussaini. The two were subsequently married and had a son, Mohammad Ali. It was rumoured that the actual father of the child was not Rustom but a blacksmith in the neighbourhood. When Rustom came to know about his wife's loose morals, he deserted her and left Lucknow. Hussaini continued with her wayward ways and became pregnant once again, ostensibly impregnated by one of the sons in the household where she worked as a menial worker. This time, she delivered a daughter, and on being dismissed by her current employer, she found employment in the royal household as she was still nursing her infant daughter.

Version 4: Next to the house of one Tarak Murad, lived a man belonging to the *kurmi* tribe. The latter once borrowed a sum of money from Tarak to buy cloth, but instead of repaying back the loan, absconded, leaving his wife and child behind. The child was about five years old, a girl named Dulari. Tarak apprehended the wife, who was not in a position to repay the loan; she preferred to sell her daughter to him, for a sum of Rs 60. When Dulari attained puberty, she developed an illicit relationship with Rustom, the son of Tarak. When the patriarch died, his family faced distress, with Dulari wandering in the bazaars and by-lanes; she formed an intimacy with a blacksmith and an elephant driver. When she gave birth to a son, Mohammad Ali, it was not clear whether the child's father was Rustom, the elephant driver or the blacksmith. By the time Mohammad Ali was three years old, Dulari gave birth to a daughter, whose parentage was again in doubt. When Munna Jaan was born in the palace, a search was conducted for a suitable wet nurse by the courtiers of Badshah Begum. Since Dulari was a young woman, and had yet not weaned her daughter, she was chosen to nurse the infant, Munna Jaan.

With Munna's origins already in doubt, Dulari, accompanied by her young son and infant daughter, entered the royal household. Nasir-ud-Din, who had a roving eye, was attracted to this wet nurse (although she was neither youthful, nor physically attractive), which rather astonished the royal court. He not only insisted on marrying Dulari, he also agreed to her wish of declaring Mohammad Ali as his legal heir, with the title Kaiwan Jah. Dulari was given the title of Mallika Zamani and all her near and dear ones from her wretched past honoured with titles and land grants. The only loser in this game was Rustom, the original husband, who was imprisoned on the instigation of Dulari. Described as an "ill-looking, low caste wretch with long, straight, lank hair, coarse falling lips and bad teeth", Kaiwan Jah started receiving the customary *nazars* (tributes / offerings) as heir apparent. Although both Kaiwan Jah and Munna Jaan were regarded as equal in rank, Kaiwan, being elder and declared as heir evidently had the upper hand. However, more was yet to come, as history was to repeat itself.

The king's roving eye now focussed on another maidservant, Qudsia, who was a maid-in-waiting for Dulari *a.k.a.* Mallika Zamani. Qudsia had humble origins — being married to Mir Haider Ali, a sitar player and having two children through him. While stories of Nasir-ud-Din being besotted with women are legend, it appears that he genuinely loved Qudsia after their marriage on December 17, 1831 and the feelings were mutual. Apparently Nasir wanted Qudsia to bear him a child who would be the true heir to the throne. As his attentions towards Mallika Zamani diminished, so did the importance of both Kaiwan Jah and Munna Jaan. The king wrote on the *arzi* (petition) of a nobleman regarding the neglect of the youth as, "Faridun Bhakt is the child of Mir Fazl Ali and Kaiwan Jah, the son of, you know who." This chaotic state of affairs in the court of Awadh was utilised to the hilt by Badshah Begum, successive *wazirs* - Agha Mir, Hakim Mehdi and Roshan-ud-Daula, and of course, the British, who played the role of the devil's advocate. Eventually, both the contenders for the throne were officially repudiated by Nasir. Kaiwan Jah died of cholera on May 16, 1838. He was buried near *Karbala Mir Khuda Baksh* at Talkatora, Lucknow. His mother built a small but elegant *Imambara* over his remains, which is still extant, but in a dilapidated condition. Kaiwan had one son, Nawab Wazir Mirza, more popularly known as Wala Qadar. A road in Old Lucknow named after Wala Qadar is still extant. Dulari or Mallika Zamani died on December 22, 1843.

Nasir had died in the night on July 7, 1837, having been poisoned to death, presumably by the hands of yet another maidservant, Dhania Mehri, at the instigation of the British. For a short time, Dhania too had wielded tremendous clout with Nasir, and had amassed a fortune, by which she is credited to have built several monuments in and around Lucknow. A bridge, *Dhania Mehri ka Pul* is still extant in Lucknow. After the untimely death of Nasir, the question of his successor cropped up, with the British being firm not to allow Munna Jaan to occupy the throne. The imperious Badshah Begum rallied forth with her armed followers, and placed Munna Jaan on the throne at *Lal Baradari*. This was stoutly opposed by the British, who forcefully ejected Badshah Begum and her followers from the throne room, arresting both the *begum* and her protégé, and confining them within the Residency. They were deported to Chunar Fort and later made to sign an undertaking to "abstain for the future, from all acts direct or indirect to create commotion or disaffection in the kingdom of Oudh.." Munna Jaan died on January 11, 1846, and the *begum* died shortly afterwards. A dismal phase in Awadh history had come to a close, but more was to follow.

The British had installed Nasir-ud-Daula, as the third king of Awadh. He was around 63 years of age at the time of his coronation by the British, being the third son of Sa'adat Ali Khan, the sixth Nawab of Awadh. This venerable old man, together with his family, consisting of his eldest son - Amjad Ali Shah, grandson Wajid Ali Shah and few others had been subjected to severe intimidation by the supporters of Badshah Begum. By a quirk of faith, he succeeded his nephew, Nasir-ud-Din Haider, and he ruled for five years (1837 - 42) as Mohammad Ali Shah Bahadur. He was aged but certainly not senile and his short tenure as ruler was not marred by any personal controversies. However, his position was challenged by three contenders: Kaiwan Jah, Munna Jaan (at the instigation of Badshah Begum again) and one Iqbal-ud-Daula, son of Shams-ud-Daula, second son of the late Sa'adat Ali Khan, who fancied himself as the true successor to the Nawabi *masnad*, mentioned earlier. Kaiwan Jah obtained the services of a maverick British officer Capt. John Williams, formerly of the EIC, to submit a memorandum to London. The petition had a catchy title, *Mirza Kaiwan Jah or the Dethroned King of Oude in Chains.* The services of the same British officer were utilised by Iqbal-ud-Daula for a similar purpose, and another scandalous document, replete with expletives was submitted, this time with the title, *The Prince of Oude, or The Claim of the Nawaub Ekbal-Ood-Dowlah Bahadur To The Throne of Oude*. As compared to Kaiwan Jah, Iqbal-ud-Daula was more forceful and chose to bombard the British with petitions, like the one below:

"I have not the presumption, my Lord, to flatter myself that I am capable of governing Oude, at present in a most deplorable state of misery, confusion, and ruin, from the negligence of its rulers. It is not unknown to me that the British Government look with an eye of compassion on this unhappy country; and if, through the kindness of Government, I may be allowed to succeed the present king, I pledge myself to do justice to the inhabitants, and accede to every wish with which your Lordship may be pleased to honour me; I will do my utmost to make the people happy, and devote my whole time and attention to this object alone."

On being informed that "it was premature at present to enter into a consideration of any claims to succeed to the throne of Oude", Iqbal-ud-Daula announced his intention to proceed to England, requesting exemption from duty on certain articles of value to be taken by him, and also arrange for funds, which could be adjusted from his assets later on. This was again denied to him as being totally inadmissible. Iqbal-ud-Daula had earlier submitted an English translation of a will originally in Persian, for consideration by the Governor General. In one of his shrill petitions, he also chose to berate Mohammad Ali Shah, who had succeeded Nasir-ud-Din Haider, through the active participation of the British:

"After the despatch of my former arzee, it is reported that the king is dead, and the Resident has placed Nusseer-ood-Dowlah, Bahadoor, upon the throne. My Lord, such a proceeding is not becoming, and in opposition to the custom of Hindoos, Mussulmen, and the English. Exclusive of the above, what can be expected from this person (Nusseer-ood-Dowlah) who is 90 years of age, blind of both eyes, and from feebleness and infirmity may be considered as alive in the grave? How will he be able to conduct the affairs of this great government? And Lucknow has now, for a long period of time, been in a desolate and unsettled state; to bring it to a proper condition it requires an able and learned chief or government, who is able of himself to arrange all matters, and keep the inhabitants contented, act up to the satisfaction of the British Government, and not to leave all affairs to his ministers. A report, prevails this day, that for some months past, Nusseer-ood-Dowlah, the present king, has been afflicted with the dropsy, and since his accession to the throne the disorder has increased to such a degree, that the usual Nuzzers presented on such have been postponed. A week has scarcely elapsed, and he is so ill; what can be expected hereafter? As all the members of this family are in hopes of succeeding to the government — by right and justice it belongs to me — bestow the government on me, or to any other member of this family who may be capable of ruling in all, wish for the restoration of prosperity, and good order in the country.

I hope what I have stated will merit your deliberate consideration, as it is an affair of importance. The succession of Nawaub Nusseer-ood-Dowlah, on account of his being the third son of the late Nawaub Saadut Allee Khan, as well as in consequence of primogeniture, his being of a sickly constitution, blind, and imbecile, is a matter of astonishment to everybody."

The British remained adamant about not entertaining the claims of Iqbal-ud-Daula. Consequently, he proceeded to London to present his case, where he was ignored once again. Realising that his claim had been finally set aside, he passed the remainder of his life as a recluse in Iraq. He was purported to have assisted the British during the Anglo-Persian War in 1856 and was consequently granted a large pension for his services. Iqbal-ud-Daula died near Baghdad, on December 21, 1887.

When Badshah Begum had been incarcerated in Chunar Fort, together with her followers and Munna Jaan, the security around her was not that strict. With time, she managed to establish contact outside the fort, through the help of her loyal followers. A solicitor of Calcutta, named Higgins sought permission from the Governor General to communicate with the *begum* and forward the claim of Munna Jaan to London. Badshah Begum paid for his services; later, it came to be known that she had been in touch with several money lenders and bankers, who were sympathetic towards her cause. By this time, Badshah Begum had been permitted to proceed for Benaras, but the events above raised the hackles of the British. All consideration and sympathy for her were promptly withdrawn and the Governor General decided to keep the *begum* and Munna Jaan incarcerated at Chunar Fort, instead of allowing them to settle in Benaras. Instructions were also passed to keep these two under strict supervision and check their contacts of doubtful integrity. Quite understandably, Mohammad Ali Shah at Lucknow also felt that by her actions, she had not only forfeited her allowance, she was to be confined to Chunar fort only. Badshah Begum and Munna Jaan were made to sign the undertaking (described above). After her death, her properties were confiscated by the then reigning king, Amjad Ali Shah. And thus ended the chequered career of Awadh's first queen.

Amjad Ali Shah, respectfully addressed as *Hazrat* (due to his pious nature), ascended the Awadh royal throne at the *Qasr us-Sultan*, more commonly known as *Lal Baradari* at Lucknow, on May 17, 1842. He had been earlier appointed as *Wali Ahad* (successor designate) on October 15, 1837, soon after his father, Mohammad Ali Shah, had succeeded Naşir-ud-Din Haider on July 7, 1837, although he was the son of his *second queen*, Jahanara Begum (Khetu Begum). Mohammad Ali Shah's first queen, Sultana Boa, a Mughal princess (daughter of Suleiman Shikoh) could not bear any offspring. Amjad Ali Shah's inheritance was pretty clear, even though he had eight brothers and five sisters. But his own succession was murky.

With the coronation of Amjad Ali Shah, Wajid Ali Shah became the heir designate or *Wali Ahad*. As part of his training in administration, young Wajid had also served as *peshkaar* (deputy or assistant, especially as in a court of law) to his father. In fact, Mustafa

Ali, the eldest son of Amjad Ali Shah, had been earlier repudiated by his father in 1838, deprived of his titles and even imprisoned, with no hope of becoming the claimant to the throne. (four decades later, his titles would be restored by the British, but this would be too little and too late). The reason behind Mustafa Ali's conflict with Amjad Ali Shah appears to have been his propensity to complain to the king (his grandfather), against his own father, about day-to-day events in the court. Historians have also surmised that Mustafa was *persona non grata* for another reason: he was not the son of *Khas Mahal*, Mallika Kishwar. But this is open to question - being the son of *Khas Mahals* gave no special privileges to princes regarding their succession, as we have already discussed in the beginning of this Chapter. Despite Amjad Ali Shah's religious bent of mind and righteous nature (he kept his own son, Wajid Ali on a short leash), the genes of his lineage came calling, and that too in old age. Initially, he became enamoured by a comely maidservant who met with an "accident" which disfigured her for life. This "accident" had been apparently engineered by Mallika Kishwar, the *Khas Mahal*. The king had his vengeance by marrying the young daughter of a fruit and flower seller, who used to bring flowers inside the palace. She was given the title of Mallika Ahad* by the king, but was not allowed to enter the palace by *Janab-e-Alia* Mallika Kishwar, even though the former later gave birth to a son. It was only during the dying moments of Amjad Ali, that mother and son were allowed to meet the ruler, with the king beseeching Mallika Kishwar to accept the young child and bring her up as her own.

Amjad Ali Shah died of a carbuncle or virulent boil on his shoulder; the date being February 13, 1847. As usual, there were eyebrows raised on the manner and nature of his unusual death;

---

* Mallika Ahad's estate stretching from the now defunct Capitol Cinema to DRM office would later constitute almost half of the *Hazratganj* we know today or British era *Huzrutgunge* / Queensway. Her palace, *Begum Kothi* was the site of a horrific battle during India's First War of Independence, detailed in another Chapter. It was later converted into a Post Office, and after Independence, demolished to make way for Janpath Market. Similarly, the estate of his fourth wife, Mallika Gheti, would make way for a warren of compact homes and commercial complexes on Hewett Road / Shivaji Marg of present day Lucknow.

assassination was suspected - the needle of suspicion pointing to Alam Ara Begum, chief consort of Wajid Ali Shah. After all, there had been previous assassination attempts on Mallika Kishwar herself, and who would benefit the most, if Mallika Kishwar died or Amjad Ali Shah was removed from the scene? But these remained conjectures. Wajid Ali Shah was anointed as the last king of Awadh on the same day, even as his father's corpse lay in state, awaiting a royal funeral. The sounds of guns firing and people cheering for the new ruler drowned the wails and lamentations for the dead ruler by his queen and her attendants.

Wajid Ali's colourful (and stormy) rule at Lucknow and depressing end at Calcutta have been described in detail by several authors and it would serve no useful purpose to reiterate the same here. However, the problem he faced was peculiar; he did not face any challenges during his ascension on February 13, 1847, but he was summarily removed by the British on February 11, 1856 after nine years of "misrule" (to coin a British term). There was no doubt that Nawabi Awadh had become a cauldron for court politics, corruption and licentious living. Or so the British surmised. But the citizens of the kingdom loved their ruler and paid back the British in their own coin by way of a violent and bloody uprising, which we now refer to as India's First War of Independence. This uprising spoilt Wajid Ali's chances of ever returning from Calcutta to Lucknow by any means (even as a British supporter), although his wives and nobleman had taken to arms and were fighting for their self respect back in Lucknow.

According to a popular urban legend of Lucknow, the British arrived at *Kaiserbagh* to "arrest" Wajid Ali; the king's courtiers and guards beat a hasty retreat but the corpulent king did not put on his footwear by himself since it was below his dignity to do so, and hence, was unable to flee. The British soldiers captured him easily and he was deported to Calcutta. Nothing can be further from the truth as this obnoxious tale, which is often narrated by "guides" to tourists visiting Lucknow's Nawabi monuments. So let us set the record straight in simple terms:

1. The "kingdom" of Awadh had long served as a buffer state between the British in the east and growing Maratha influence

in north India. The Governor General at Calcutta now wanted direct control over Awadh's riches and military might, instead of dealing through a succession of Residents and recalcitrant Nawabs (later "kings").

2. Military successes of the British in other parts of the Indian sub-continent had made them over-confident and foolhardy.
3. Policies such as Doctrine of Lapse (e.g. Jhansi) or direct military offensive (e.g. Mysore / Seringapatam) were not applicable on Awadh, since by all practical purposes, the rulers of Awadh were British supporters and there had never been any conflict between Calcutta and Lucknow after Shuja-ud-Daula's defeat at the Buxar (despite the constant undercurrent of tension between successive Nawabi rulers and British Residents).
4. The British tried to coax and cajole and even threaten Wajid Ali to abdicate, on the grounds of "extensive misrule", "cruel oppression which prevailed throughout His Majesty's dominions", the "deplorable condition of Oude (Awadh)" as a whole and "ill-health" of the king himself. The latter was offered a substantial pension, the *Dilkusha* palace to settle down with his retinue and enjoy the remainder of his life with his wives and titles, devoid of any authority or responsibility.
5. As evident from the despatches between Calcutta and Lucknow, the East India Company in Calcutta with its Court of Directors at London, had already started using the terms "British Government" and "Government of India" interchangeably with itself, although neither the Crown nor British Parliament were *directly* involved in the Company's machinations in the Indian sub-continent. Extracts of instructions January 23, 1856) to Outram (the officiating Resident at Lucknow) from Calcutta are quite revealing:
    - *The Governor General in Council having thereupon resolved to proceed at once to the establishment of the new policy which he had proposed, and to carry into effect the instructions of the Honourable Court for the assumption of the Government of Oude....*

- *You will point out to the Minister* (Ali Naqi Khan, Prime Minister of Awadh) *that the resolution of the British Government to assume forthwith the administration of Oude, in one form or the other, has been finally taken, and is inflexible...*
- *The Resident will inform the King .... the Governor General has instructed him to state, that the resolution of the Government of India is irrevocably taken...*

6. Against the face of such insurmountable odds, Wajid Ali proved to be surprisingly adamant about retaining his titles/position and all attempts by the British to take control of Awadh started floundering. As per plan, the British next issued an ultimatum that either the king should sign on the Draft Treaty which was basically an instrument of accession within three days, or the Governor General would anyhow, assume control of Oude (Awadh), but in that case, the British would not provide guarantees, as regards the king's titles, payment of stipend or personal security.
7. Without signing any document or "Treaty", Wajid Ali simply walked out of his palace, urging his citizens to keep calm and not to revert to arms or violence. He planned to meet the Governor General at Calcutta and eventually reach London to petition Queen Victoria. However, this would involve a long and arduous journey by river and sea, which he had not taken into account.
8. The British quickly stepped into the political and administrative vacuum created by Wajid Ali's departure from Lucknow and tried their best to introduce their own model of governance, which would prove to be a failure.

Wajid Ali was an unwelcome guest (not a prisoner or an exile) at Calcutta. His retinue consisted of the dowager queen, Mallika Kishwar, Alam Ara Begum, his *Khas Mahal*, four or five other *begums*, Mirza Sikandar Hashmat, his brother, Mohammad Hamid Ali, *Wali Ahad* (heir apparent) and several courtiers. People from his Lucknow court also started flocking to Calcutta to be with their beloved king, and his establishment soon started burgeoning, putting strain on his finances. Wajid Ali's physical condition did not permit him to undertake a long and arduous journey across the seas and in a change of strategy, it was decided that Mallika Kishwar would petition the Queen at London. Among others, she was accompanied by Sikandar Hashmat, Hamid Ali and British lobbyists, Captain Robert Bird and John Brandon. On the 4th of July, 1857, Mallika Kishwar finally met Queen Victoria at Buckingham Palace, London. The former was not aware that the British Monarch had no power to reverse Wajid Ali's deposition. Also, by that time, the uprising had broken out in the Indian sub-continent, and the *begum's* contingent had lost whatever initial sympathy it had garnered among the British public. Her delegation and effort were doomed and so was Awadh.

Fig. 1: Awadh entourage in London (1857), Unidentified Photographer.

During their return journey, Mallika Kishwar and Sikandar Hashmat passed away in Paris. When Hamid Ali eventually made it back to Calcutta, he did so as a prince without a realm because the British had already decided that upon Wajid Ali's death, his royal title would dissolve and his descendants would no longer be regarded as royalty. After all, the British had conferred kingship onto Ghazi-ud-Din Haider, ratifying it for each consecutive "ruler." Therefore, it was also their right to end this elaborate charade whenever they deemed it fit to do so. Wajid Ali died on September 21, 1887, sparking off an ongoing, acrimonious dispute on who would inherit his titles and possessions. However, for all practical purposes, with Wajid Ali's demise, the lineage of Burhan-ul-Mulk and Awadh's colourful phase had come to an end.

Chapter - II

The Recalcitrant Begum

Historical Background

The rulers of Awadh, like other Islamic rulers of that medieval age, had the propensity to enter into wedlock a number of times. It is emphasised here that Safdar Jang, the second Nawab Wazir of Awadh, remained faithful to Sadr-e-Jahan, popularly known as Nawab Begum. She was the daughter of Sa'adat Khan Burhan-ul-Mulk, the first Nawab Wazir of Awadh. Safdar Jang was the nephew and son-in-law of Burhan-ul-Mulk. Unlike his predecessor or successors, Safdar Jang did not maintain a harem. For the rulers of Awadh, the chief consort or *Khas Mahal* would invariably have her origins from a noble / accomplished family, through an arranged *nikah* marriage, sometimes even arranged for by the Mughal Emperor himself. As the chief consort (later principal queen) of the ruler, her position was assured in the Nawabi court, whether she enjoyed cordial relations with the ruler or not. Other junior wives or *khurd begums* would come via the *mut'ah* (an ancient Islamic practice of uniting man and woman as husband and wife, for a limited time, on mutual agreement) route; they could be of any origin - from daughters of nobleman to maids-in-waiting and even dancers and women of doubtful virtue. However, an unfortunate aspect of these sexual dynamics within the Nawabi *zenana* was that after the death of a ruler, the members of his harem faced loss of status and possibly penury. More often than not, the new ruler would not only choose to ignore the women folk of the former ruler, he would be prone to look upon them with suspicion and wariness. This is because some of the *begums*, particularly the *Khas Mahals* would be inclined to play court politics from within the *zenana*. The financial independence of these *begums* lay in the dowries they received at the time of their marriage. Some dowries were legendary in size, while some, a mere pittance. Among the *begums* of Awadh, Nawab Begum, and even more so, her daughter-in-law, Bahu Begum, happened to be extremely rich women in their own right. Not only did their dowries consist of invaluable jewellery, gold, silver, clothes, elaborate household effects, horses, elephants, cattle, servants, a token army, but also of villages and indeed entire districts. Legally, this was always their property and not that of their husbands. The land provided them with revenue throughout their lives. Apart from this dowry, an appropriate *mehar* was fixed at the time of marriage which could be claimed by the wife from her husband at any time. Even though this *mehar* was rarely claimed, it was part of Islamic jurisprudence and was far from being just an empty formality.

Some *begums* like Bahu Begum, the widow of Shuja-ud-Daula, Badshah Begum, the widow of Ghazi-ud-Din Haider and Mallika Kishwar, the widow of Amjad Ali Shah, even played the role of king maker, due to the tremendous clout they enjoyed in court politics, and their personal fortunes and estates which enabled them to run an almost parallel administration in the Nawabi court. The less fortunate *khurd begums* (or *mahals*, if they had given birth to sons) lived the rest of their lives in anonymity and deprivation, staying in lesser, abandoned palaces, while the new ruler built a palace for himself and his establishment. The British too did not follow any fair or uniform policy regarding the widows of the Awadh rulers; the former were constantly on a look-out to score brownie points against the Nawabi court and indulge in petty politics, which originated from the Governor General's table in Calcutta and seeped down to the Resident's establishment in Lucknow.

We have seen in the previous Chapter how complicated the succession pattern could be in the Nawabi court of Lucknow. However, the purpose of this Chapter is not to discuss the harems of Awadh rulers and the gender dynamics therein, but to describe the lone but spirited fight of a *Khas Mahal* for her rights and estates, after the demise of her husband - a *begum* whom history has all but forgotten.

Shams un-Nisan (Dulhan Begum)

As discussed elsewhere, Shuja-ud-Daula had reservations in anointing his eldest son, Asaf-ud-Daula (Mirza Amani) as his successor; he was more inclined towards his second son, Sa'adat Ali Khan (Mirza Mangli), but Bahu Begum managed to have her way (see above) and Asaf-ud-Daula became the fourth Nawab Wazir of Awadh in 1775, after the death of his father. Asaf-ud-Daula promptly ordered Sa'adat Ali, then Governor of Rohilkhand to present himself with his troops; the latter preferred to stay away and reside in Benaras under British protection till more favourable times presented themselves (and they did). Shuja's third son, Azad-ud-Daula (Mirza Jangli) was a joint governor of Khairabad since 1767, away from the politics of Faizabad and Lucknow. Muin-ud-Daula (Mirza Mendhu), the fourth son of Shuja was a poet in his own right with a *nom de plume* of *Amir,* a person without any political ambitions. The purpose of detailing this genealogy will become clearer as the narrative in this Chapter progresses.

When Asaf-ud-Daula ascended the *masnad* of Awadh in 1775, he was already married to Shams un-Nisan (Dulhan Begum), whom he had married in 1770; the *begum* was the daughter of late Intizam-ud-Daula, sometime *Wazir* (Prime Minister) and also *Bakshi* (paymaster) in the Mughal court. The marriage had been arranged by her grandmother, Begum Sholapuri and her brother, Imam-ud-Din Khan. The wedding arrangements had been an elaborate affair, with Shuja spending rupees 24 lakhs on the auspicious event at Faizabad. The wedding has been described thus (Srivastava, 1945):

"*As the date approached near, elaborate arrangements were made to celebrate it in a befitting manner. On 6th November 1770 sachaq* (wedding gifts from bridegroom's side) *was sent to the house of Sholapuri Begum* (then residing in Faizabad) *in a grand procession composed of gorgeously dressed officers and well-accoutred and well-mounted troops, besides a concourse of public, with numerous valuable articles displayed for public gaze, notable among which were five thousand vessels, many of them made of silver, and many thousand trays full of sweets, bottles of perfumes, costly wearing apparel and jewels and ornaments. On the 9th mahdi* (sic) *came from the bride's house to that of the bridegroom, and on the 10th the bridegroom, then aged twenty, and party with all the pomp and display known to the eighteenth century Indian nobility marched to the bride's residence and the marriage was performed with due solemnities. The bride entered into the Nawab's palace on the 12th amidst showers of silver coins that were thrown across her palanquin to the beggars down below. It is said that Shuja spent twenty four lakhs of rupees on this happy occasion."*

The bride came from a family of illustrious Turani noblemen having origins in Central Asia, and practiced *Sunni* faith; the bridegroom was of Persian origin, and a *Shia*. The wedding ceremony had been attended by the Mughal Emperor, Shah Alam - II and his courtiers. This cross-cultural marriage could have had great political significance; unfortunately, it came to naught. Shams un-Nisan, who stayed in the *Macchi Bhavan* palace at Lucknow had to handle a failed marriage with Asaf-ud-Daula, who showed no interest in her, but even greater misfortunes were in store for this unfortunate *Khas Mahal,* as time would tell.

Asaf-ud-Daula died in 1797 and was succeeded by Wazir Ali Khan, whose innings lasted for a mere six months, before he was deposed and replaced by Sa'adat Ali Khan in 1798. The new Nawab Wazir seemed to have issues with both Bahu Begum, the mother of Asaf-ud-Daula, who had initially resisted against his candidature for the *masnad,* as well as with Shams un-Nisan, the widow of Asaf-ud-Daula, whom he respectfully addressed as Bhabi Begum. He also resented the fact that his own mother did not enjoy the respect and regard due to her, because Bahu Begum continued to run her writ from Faizabad. Observing the changed political scenario, Bahu Begum capitulated and assured full support to Sa'adat Ali, but Shams un-Nisan was made of sterner stuff. It has been suggested by some writers that the new Nawab confiscated some of Shams un-Nisan's revenues, and ignored her wishes, asserting himself as the new ruler and master, but this premise has not been substantiated. Whatever might have been the reason, as her outrage and resentment mounted with time, the widowed *begum*, Shams un-Nisan petitioned the British with her litany of grievances, expressing her desire to leave Awadh and settle down somewhere in the Company's territories, preferably Elahabad (Allahabad). When this news reached Sa'adat Ali Khan, he was understandably appalled, but the British, led by John Baillie, the Resident at Lucknow, seemed to have played the devil's advocate in the imbroglio.

That something was not quite right with Sa'adat Khan's relations with his immediate family members can be gauged from the fact that Azad ud-Daula *a.k.a.* Mirza Jangli (see above), had returned to Lucknow in 1793 during Asaf-ud-Daula's reign, only to be expelled from the city in 1807. He then settled in Patna under British protection, where he was granted a large monthly pension and landed properties. Mirza Jangli was later granted the *jagir* of Sarvan, in Jhansi, by Maharaja Mahadji Scindia. Muin-ud-Daula *a.k.a.* Mirza Mendhu, the poet, who had also settled in Lucknow was also expelled in 1807; he too preferred to settle in Patna under British protection, where he was granted a substantial monthly pension and landed properties. Sa'adat Ali was also in constant conflict with Bahu Begum, was well as the junior *khurd begums / mahals* of the late Shuja *viz.* Gori Begum, Zeb un-Nisan Khanum, Bibi Faizi, Jani Begum, Mukhoo Begum, Ashraf un-Nisan, Zeenat un-Nisan, Hayati Begum, Najm un-Nisan, Hussain Bai, Misri Khanum, Hussaini Begum, Fakhr un-Nisan and several others. One of the petitions of the impoverished *begums* ran thus:

"Our rent garments complain of our hands. The skirts of our robe complain of the tears we shed. So long we have been confined in the dungeon of sorrow, our very chains are fretted and our prison complains of us. No prospect of life remains to us. Perhaps the holy martyrs of the plain of Karbala, and the wretched captives of the desert of calamity and woe, may come to the succour of us, wretched and afflicted sufferers. Enough, enough! May God cause the sun of your life and prosperity ever to continue refulgent."

So what was the reason behind this sorry state of affairs of the *khurd mahals*? After the demise of Shuja-ud-Daula, Asaf-ud-Daula had segregated Bahu Begum from the *khurd mahals*, as regards their maintenance. Bahu Begum had her own estates from where she obtained substantial revenue. A separate department was created for providing stipends to the *khurd mahals*. Even material gifts were segregated between Bahu Begum and the lesser *mahals*. After Sa'adat Khan ascended the *masnad*, an order was passed that the stipends would be released on an annual basis. This encouraged Tahseen Ali Khan, a *nazir* (court official), responsible for disbursing the stipends, to deduct three percent from the payments made; bribery also became rampant and as the *nazir* became increasingly brazen with time, he started oppressing the junior *mahals* by various ways and means. Due to his actions and inactions, Tahseen was removed, but managed to get Nukhut, who was his protégé, as *daroga*. On seeing the worsening situation, the junior *mahals* tried to petition the Nawab in person but were rebuffed. In the meantime, they were confined within their palace and subject to severe deprivation under the instructions of Tahseen and his flunkies, who apparently also had the support of Bahu Begum. Sa'adat Ali, it seems, remained blissfully unaware of the situation at Faizabad, although the junior *mahals* continue to petition him and the British for relief.

To come back to the trials and tribulations of Shams un-Nisan, on September 1, 1812, John Baillie, the Resident of Lucknow informed Neil Edmonstone, then Chief Secretary, that Shams un-Nisan had finally left Lucknow and proceeded to her *jagir* at Pertaubghur (Pratapgarh) a distance of 12 *kos* away from the city (1 *kos* = approx 3.2 km) with the intention of staying there for a short time, and then proceeding to British territory, where her residence may be fixed. He also informed that Sa'adat Ali had sent a conciliatory letter to his sister-in-law, which she had refused to open. In the letter, Sa'adat Ali had reminded the *begum* that her leaving the city was improper and unbecoming, an occurrence which had never happened before. He had reiterated that people of all denominations respected her in her own country, but it would not be so in another country. Sa'adat had concluded his letter with the following entreaty:

"I request your Highness to desist from this design, and to relinquish your hasty resolution. I am ready to serve you in every possible way; and if you agree to this proposal of mine, I shall attend you, and repeat the assurances in person. What can I say more?"

However, the *begum* remained adamant, but on Baillie's entreaties, she had agreed to postpone her journey, when actually she proceeded anyhow. Edmonstone responded that the prospect of any reconciliation between Sa'adat Ali and the *begum* appeared to be remote. He also pointed out the fact that the running feud between the two had been going on for a long time now; earlier the *begum* had proposed that she may be allowed to proceed on pilgrimage to *Karbala,* and that the earnings from her *jagir* should be remitted to her, after collection by her own servants. Another long-standing demand of the *begum* was that the provisions supplied to her from the Nawab's kitchen be commuted for an annual payment to be remitted to her.

By October 1812, the *begum* upped the ante by demanding that the dues accruing to her be remitted to her regularly through the British government, irrespective of where she finally resided. And more importantly, these dues should also include the incomes from her hereditary properties in and around Delhi. She also expressed her desire to finally settle in Allahabad or Patna, after her final departure from her *jagir* at Pratapgarh on November 13 - 14, 1812. Although the British capitulated to her wishes and agreed to provide her with the necessary protection and regard, befitting her rank and status, more was yet to come. Sa'adat Ali had not been idle and had demanded a true valuation of the *begum*'s *jagir*, together with authentic documents for determining the revenue generated from it. After the *begum* finally arrived at Allahabad on December 16, 1813, she protested vehemently against this clause of Sa'adat Ali, and threatened to proceed to Calcutta and petition the Governor General in person. In fact, she had already sent a long and detailed prayer addressed to the Governor General, in which she had given details of the persecution and maltreatment meted out to her. Surprisingly, in her *arzi* (petition), she had also included her brother, (late) Imam-ud-Din Khan (mentioned earlier), as one who were equally responsible for her sad state of affairs. The claim for her hereditary properties in and around Delhi were as follows:

- Sheikhpur
- Badarpur
- Mukundpur
- Qamar-ud-Din Nagar
- Noorpur
- Mamoorpur
- Sai Maharajpur
- Wazirpur
- Naurzopur
- Janpur
- Mudowleh
- Kore Kukur

- The houses of Debi Dutt and Yakub Khan
- The houses of Itmād-ud-Daula Bahadur
- The houses of Nawab Alia Sholapuri Begum (her grandmother)
- The houses of Murtaza Khan
- The garden of Yakub Khan
- The garden of Ihtemām Khan
- The garden of Qazi Ekrām
- The garden of Kokultash Khan
- The garden of Chak Mubaraqpur
- The garden of Rasheed Khan
- The garden Mulk Dhuka, Chak Sudora, Charbagh of Itmād-ud-Daula
- Wells at Budrein and Firozabad
- Some ground within the house of Nawab Qumar-ud-Din Khan on the bank of the river
- *Maqbara* (mausoleum) of Qumar-ud-Din Khan
- The village of Mubdsheer, commonly called Qasbah Burrum
- A garden near the *nullah* (drain) of Syed Hamid Khan
- Faiz Bari, a garden
- Ghose Pur, a garden
- Retio (*sic*), a garden
- Mutchee Bhuvan (*sic*) and the stables of Dara Shikoh, formerly in the possession of Itmād-ud-Daula Bahadur

In the meantime, Sa'adat Ali also hardened his stand, by flatly refusing to personally placate the estranged *begum*; he also reported to the Resident that a son-in-law of the Nawab had met her and implored her to return, but was not taken note of, nor paid any attention to whatsoever. The Nawab was also of the view that his responsibilities towards the welfare of his sister-in-law ceased on the day she crossed over to live in the Company's territory and accordingly no allowance would now be due to her. Sa'adat adroitly pointed out that he was not in possession of the *begum*'s properties at Delhi; also the claim for those properties would legally rest on her brother, Imam-ud-Din

Khan, now deceased, and after him, to her nephew Hussain-ud-Din Khan. That the *begum* could not solely assert a claim to the proprietary right of those assets. The Nawab further asserted that the *begum* was being misguided by certain vested interests and the decisions taken by her were not her own.

Shams un-Nisan Dulhan Begum died at Allahabad, shortly after settling there. Her remains were brought to Lucknow and interred in the *Asafi* or *"Bada" Imambada*, adjacent to the humble grave of her husband, Asaf-ud-Daula. The credit for this final act of sentiment goes to Ghazi-ud-Din Haider, who succeeded Sa'adat Ali Khan as Nawab Wazir in 1814.

Chapter - III

La connexion Française (The French Connection)

Historical Background

The British East India Company is well known in India for its marauding activities, soon after they landed at the port of Surat in the Indian sub-continent on August 24, 1608, ostensibly to trade in spices. The Portuguese (1505) had reached India more than a century before the British and the Dutch (1604), although they remained confined to pockets and did not have a pan-Indian presence. The French East India Company (French*: Compagnie Française pour le commerce des Indes Orientales*) was founded on September 1, 1664 to compete with the English (later British) and Dutch trading companies in the East Indies. It obtained a royal mandate from Mughal Emperor Aurangzeb for trade; however it was soon embroiled in hostilities with the British, which was a spill-over from its rivalries with the latter in Europe. The French had a substantial presence in the trading ports of Pondicherry and Chandernagore. The French Governor General, Joseph Francois Dupleix continued on an active and aggressive policy against the British, including the forging of alliances with rulers in the Deccan (south India), until he was recalled to Paris in 1754.

Ironically, the presence of French soldiers in India and their military prowess have often been downplayed by writers; the former were often referred to deprecatingly as *military adventurers* as if their presence and motives were inconsequential and wholly mercenary in nature. But a closer look at the political scenario of the Indian sub-continent in the eighteenth century reveals a different picture altogether. The powerful Mughal empire was waning, slowly being transformed into a "pale shadow of its former glory" as regional power centres, that included Awadh in particular, assumed importance. Zahir-ud-Din Babur had won the First Battle of Panipat in 1526 and laid the foundations of the Mughal empire in India. The battle had been won on the strength of gunpowder firearms and field artillery, but Babur's successors showed no inclination in modernising their forces, in terms of firearms and battle strategies. This resulted in the frequent routing of Mughal forces, who, although vast in numbers, fell short of adopting modern methods of warfare. Having seen the consequences of the Battle of Plassey (1757) and the Battle of Buxar (1764), which established British rule in India, Shuja-ud-Daula, the reigning Nawab of Awadh, although defeated by the former, continued to make efforts to modernise and strengthen his army, and he was not averse to hiring French soldiers to assist him in this task.

Even before the Battle of Buxar, Shuja-ud-Daula had made overtures to Law de Lauriston in 1757 to help in modernising the Awadh forces. Lauriston, who was Governor of Pondicherry for two terms, would later rebuild Pondicherry in 1765; the town had been reduced to ruins by the British in 1761. In due course of time, many French soldiers preferred to look for greener pastures, after quitting Company service. The most prominent of these were Chevaliar René Madec, Walter Reinhardt Sombre, Benoît de Boigne, Pierre Cuillier-Perron (Piron), Etienne Pedron, Antoine Polier, Jean Baptiste Joseph Gentil and of course, Claude Martin.

But what made the French seek employment with Indian rulers (and even with the British at times) so readily? To understand this conundrum, we need to look into the individual dynamics that existed within the British East India Company and the French East India Company. The British EIC was founded in 1600 and went through several formative *avatars*, before being dissolved in 1874. Ostensibly created for trade in the far east, its predatory tactics and political aspirations resulted in Company ownership or "rule" over large tracts of land within the Indian sub-continent. Its army, although poorly paid, was larger than the British army. Being a joint-stock Company, the EIC enjoyed the support of the Monarch and Parliament back in London; it also enjoyed the imperial patronage of the Mughal rulers, including Jahangir and Shah Jahan, although cracks had started appearing in this ideal scenario from the rule of Aurangzeb onwards. The EIC not only enjoyed a monopoly in its trade with India, its employees also engaged in private business deals, many becoming extremely wealthy in due course of time.

The French East India Company was founded in 1664, although it had its origins from earlier *Compagnie des Indes Orientales*, from 1604 onwards. It was not a joint-stock corporation, but was funded by the Crown - notably Henry IV to Louis XIV. Britain was a constitutional monarchy, France an absolute monarchy. This meant that there were legal differences in who / what the companies were responsible to. The English (later British) East India Company was responsible to the British Parliament. The French Company had no such legislature to answer to. Moreover, due to the War of Spanish Succession (1701 - 1704), the Company did not get patronage from the royal court and went on a path of bankruptcy. In any case, France saw more profits from the West Indies, as compared to the East Indies. The French Revolution hastened the Company's decline, and it was liquidated in 1794. In India, it fought several battles with the British; its lack of naval strength contributed to its defeat, resulting in the loss of settlements of Pondicherry and Chandernagore to their chief rival, the British. Unlike the British EIC, which enforced severe restrictions on its soldiers, preventing them from offering their services to native rulers, the French EIC had no such impositions. After humiliating defeats at the hands of the British, French soldiers faced penury, humiliation and unemployment, forcing them to migrate to greener pastures. Even while in active service, French EIC soldiers remained unpaid for long periods due to financial constraints of the parent Company. Some French soldiers preferred to join the British, but here too, they faced loss of rank, discrimination and reduction in pay. Hence, the only options available to them were either to return to France or join the services of Indian rulers - the latter being more lucrative and attractive, due to obvious reasons. There were also instances of French soldiers having returned to their homeland, facing unemployment and then, reverting back to India to join the services of a native ruler.

The Enigmatic "Adventurers"

Benoît de Boigne (Benoit La Borgne) was born on March 8, 1751 at Chambéry, France. His family was of modest means, and the young boy's ambition at an early age was to enlist in the French army and serve his motherland. Failing to obtain a commission, he left France and joined the Irish Brigade, but was soon disillusioned, due to lack of professional growth and the meagre pay of a subaltern. Some would say that he was a mercenary at heart, as he had no qualms in quitting his assignment and joining the Russian army, under Admiral Orloff, then stationed in Greece and heading the forces of Empress Catherine II. His satisfaction was short-lived however, as his regiment suffered a humiliating defeat at the hands of the Turks and he was taken prisoner. After many travails, he managed to petition Empress Catherine and return to active service. In due course of time, he came to know about the opportunities in the Indian sub-continent, and managed a letter of introduction to Warren Hastings in the Bengal Presidency. De Boigne landed on Indian shores on 1778, then a strapping young man, 27 years of age.

He joined British service as a subaltern, in the 6th Regiment of the Madras Native Infantry. This desperate move was fuelled by the fact that back in Europe, war had been declared between England and France, Pondicherry was under siege by Sir Hector Munro, and De Boigne's own slender resources had been exhausted due to his long period of unemployment in a foreign country. But he was soon weary of his own pointless existence, and coupled with certain serious charges levelled against him, which made him resign his commission and reach Calcutta to meet Warren Hastings, the Governor General. Armed with letters of introduction, he proceeded to Awadh in 1783 and joined the services of Nathaniel Middleton, who was completing his third term as Resident of Lucknow. Asaf-ud-Daula had already shifted his capital from Faizabad to Lucknow and the former received the Frenchman courteously, presenting him with a *khillat* (ceremonial robe of honour). De Boigne settled in Lucknow and studied local languages, also making suitable preparations for his onward journey to Afghanistan.

After leaving Lucknow in due course of time, De Boigne decided to pay his respects to the Mughal court, before proceeding further in his journey, but was treated coldly and disdainfully by Mirza Shafi, the *Wazir* of Shah Alam. The Marathas who were camped near Agra, invited De Boigne, although both the Mughal and the Maratha camps looked upon the Frenchman with suspicion, because he was after all, a representative of the EIC. De Boigne's baggage was looted during his march. The plunder of his money, maps and plans was a serious setback for this intrepid French soldier, but he decided to face his fate resolutely, proposing to raise a battalion and offer its services to the Rana of Gohad, the arch enemy of the Scindia (Maratha) camp. So here was the real irony: a Frenchman, a protégé of Warren Hastings, the British Governor General, offering his services to a native Indian ruler. De Boigne was ordered to return to Calcutta immediately. The Frenchman complied and Warren Hastings permitted him to accompany him to Lucknow, where the former was on a mission to twist the arm of Nawab Asaf-ud-Daula, for reforms and money.

In the meantime, the Maratha leader, Madhoji Scindia had not been idle. He had kept tabs on the career and exploits of De Boigne and concluded that it would be better to have this intrepid Frenchman on his side, than have him in the enemy camp. He offered a commission to De Boigne, which the latter accepted and set about his task with energy and enthusiasm, creating two battalions for the Maratha forces, within five months. This enabled Scindia to become a king maker at Delhi, propping up Shah Alam as the Emperor with Maratha support. De Boigne had arrived in the northern plains of India during the times of Asaf-ud-Daula; hence he found no employment in Awadh as a military expert and strategist. Although his elite brigades remained in the service of the Marathas, he did not get the honour or career progression which he rightly deserved, due to a variety of reasons, mostly political and strategic. However, he continued to visit Lucknow and meet his close friend Claude Martin, who, by then, was firmly ensconced in the Awadh court, as more of a businessman and wheeler-dealer than as a military advisor. For some time, he went into a business partnership with Martin, for the manufacture of indigo. Finally, De Boigne left India for France in September 1796, leaving behind his troopers who were eventually transferred under the command of Asaf-ud-Daula at Lucknow. He died on June 21, 1830.

General Perron (Pierre Cuillier) was born in Sarthe, France on August 6, 1753. The son of a failed businessman, he acquired the mastery of casting cannons in a foundry at Nantes. He arrived in India aboard the French frigate, *Sardine*, but preferred to desert his ship, and land on the coast of Malabar, with three other deserters. Journeying to the northern plains of India, he managed to secure employment in the foundry of the Rana of Gohad (present day Bhind district of Madhya Pradesh, near Gwalior), under the command of a Scotsman called Sangster. Discarding his patriarchal name, he assumed the pseudonym of Perron, by which he would be referred to in history. Later, he joined the services of the Raja of Bharatpur, as Quarter Master, under the command of a Frenchman, Lestineau. After the latter's forces were disbanded, Perron remained unemployed for some time, his efforts to join the Scindias and then Begum Samru, coming to naught.

Perron had been noticed by De Boigne, and the former was appointed in a new brigade at Burhanpur. Although he possessed non of the *charisma* of De Boigne, he displayed his military skills in a remarkable manner in Ajmer and Kanaund (present day Rewari district). Perron also conducted himself bravely in the battle between the Nizam of Hyderabad and the *Peshwa*'s forces. It is another matter that the Nizam's forces were under the command of Col. Richmond, another Frenchman. With time, Perron enjoyed the complete confidence of the Marathas, being authorised to raise armies, and to retain or discharge troops at will. He even sent presents to Maharaja Ranjit Singh, with proposals for a treaty of amity and friendship, which was declined politely. With time and a flurry of military successes, Perron was now commanding an army of 40,000 men. His personal income and assets grew by leaps and bounds, and so did his vanity. Reverses and conspiracies against him were to follow soon, with the Frenchman ultimately approaching Daulat Rao Scindia's camp, laying down his sword and asking for a discharge, having no desire to be "disgraced by dissolute knaves and bullies" of the Maratha court. Later, when Perron had tendered a formal resignation to Scindia, he applied to General Lake, British Commander-in-Chief at Cawnpore (Kanpur), for leave to proceed to Lucknow, with an escort of 200 cavalry and 400 infantry, on his return journey for Europe. The British were no doubt overjoyed on learning about

Perron's imminent departure; it presented them an opportunity to seize Perron's vast estates and also take Shah Alam in their protection (till now the Mughal king had been under Perron's "custody"). In due course, although Perron's armed escort was allowed and his safe conduct through Lucknow was permitted, he was essentially a fugitive on the run, with none of the power and prestige he had enjoyed until recently.

Perron reached Lucknow on October 1, 1803, under strict instructions from Wellesley to William Scott, the Resident at Lucknow that the French officer be accorded due respect and distinction as per his rank in the Maratha forces; however, his departure to Calcutta, *en route* to Europe was to be "hastened." From Lucknow, Perron reached Chandernagore, the French settlement near Calcutta; he left for Europe in September 1805, with a large fortune. He died in Fresnes, France on May 21, 1834. Perron's life was truly a rags-to-riches story in the history of French "adventurers" of India. But many would also like to call him a "soldier of misfortune" although he had been honoured with the Imperial title of "General Perron Bahadur Muzzafar Jang, Intizam-ud-daula, Nasirul-Mulk" along with *mansab* of *haft hazarii* (commander of seven thousand soldiers). On the zenith of his career, General Perron was the military in charge of the forts at Agra, Aligarh, Ajmer, Khurja, Delhi, Saharanpur, and Firozabad. A pyramid shaped tomb, with the bodies of four children of Perron interred inside is extant in the old Catholic Cemetery of the Civil Lines at Agra. It is believed that the tomb is from the 1790s, although no one knows what the children died of. Perron's own grave in France does not mention "Perron." After all, his real title was Cuillier.

Colonel (Etienne) Pedron was a native of Hennebont, near Lorient, France. He served in Law's corps at Lucknow in 1760. Formerly, he had been at Chandernagore, but had reached Lucknow before the French settlement was sacked by the British. Later, under British pressure, many Frenchmen were sacked from the Nawabi court, and among them was Pedron, who took employment under the ruler of Berar (in present day Maharashtra state). Later, he entered the services of De Boigne as Lieutenant of the First Brigade, and subsequently promoted as Commander of the Third Brigade in 1795. In 1799, he was engaged in the siege of Delhi; by 1800, Pedron raised the Fourth Brigade, due to the impending invasion by Zaman Shah (which never occurred). It has been conjectured that Pedron's victories was more due to his propensity to win over rebel factions through bribery (lure of gold) than actual military acumen.

He strengthened the fortification at Aligarh, making it a great military arsenal, but in 1803, under the onslaught of the British, he was wont to surrender, rather than heed to his chief's (Perron) exhortation to "hold the place while one stone remained upon another." Pedron was confined by his own troops, and his command replaced by Baji Rao. Aligarh was stormed on September 4, 1803, and Pedron was taken prisoner of war by the British, together with 281 captured guns. There are no more accounts of Pedron's exploits subsequent to his defeat at Aligarh, other than he was sent to Calcutta as a prisoner of war by the British.

Henri Polier: Antoine-Louis Henri de Polier, born in 1741 to Jacques H.E. Polier at Lusanne, Switzerland, was actually of French origin and an engineer by profession. He reached Indian shores in 1757 and worked as Assistant Engineer to the British EIC at Calcutta. By 1762, he had become Chief Engineer of the Bengal Army in Calcutta and had begun working on the design and construction of the new Fort William. However, due to his nationality, he saw limited career options within the EIC and therefore resigned. Warren Hasting arranged for him to go to Awadh to work for Shuja-ud-Daula at Faizabad in 1773. Later, he worked in the court of Shah Alam – II at Delhi. When the Mughals had been unable to capture Agra fort held by the Jats, despite a prolonged siege, Polier was sent to Agra by Shuja-ud-Daula, with only one contingent of the Awadh army, to aid the Mughals. Polier discarded the attack by small cannons, preferring the use of larger cannons to bombard the enemy. He did not have faith in the low calibre, limited range guns used by the Mughals, together with catapults during siege operations. Polier built entrenchments along the walls of the fort and carried out the assault with heavy guns, forcing the Jats to come to the negotiating table. The fort of Agra fell to the Mughal army on February 18, 1774.

Despite being a Frenchman and his record of military success, the Mughals remained ambivalent and cautious about Polier, due to his close connections with the British and Warren Hastings in particular. It has been suggested that Polier was part of the espionage system of the British EIC and that he was instrumental in collecting and passing on information about the political dynamics of north India to the Company. This, he carried out through his network of informers, particularly in Awadh. In fact, his very appointment in Shuja-ud-Daula's service in the capacity of Chief Architect and Engineer, was due to the fact that he was much more pliable to the British cause, than any other Frenchman, whom Shuja would have otherwise employed. Thus, under Mughal service, the peaceful *jagir* (estate) of Khalilganj was given to him to administer, together with the *jagir* of Khair (Koil); unlike Sombre and Madec, who were always in the forefront of armed skirmishes and military campaigns on behalf of the Mughals, Polier remained as more of a revenue collector and administrator than a military strategist. After the death of Shuja-ud-Daula in 1775, the British exerted tremendous pressure to dismiss all French nationals working in the Nawabi Court. Asaf-ud-Daula heeded to the Company directives, with the exception of Gentil. Polier was dismissed from the service from the Nawabi court in 1782, but was asked by Warren Hastings to remain in Lucknow as an appointee of the Company with the honorary rank of Lieutenant Colonel, as Polier's knowledge of Awadh was considered essential to the Company's interests.

While in India, Polier became an ardent collector of rare Indian antiques. He collected Persian and Sanskrit manuscripts and Indian miniatures, and possessed a complete collection of the *Vedas* (perhaps the first European in history to do so). His collection began with a gift of three albums given to him in 1767, which inspired him to further assemble *muraqqas* (albums in book form containing miniature paintings and calligraphic annotations), depicting scenes of Indian life, portraits of rulers, courtesans, architectural monuments and Hindu mythological elements. He amassed the best antique work he could find, refurbished them and also commissioned new work, principally through his favoured retained artist, Mihr Chand - the latter being largely responsible for arranging the layout and decoration of the albums made for Polier's personal collection. A distinctive mount with a broad band of naturalistic flowers between two narrow borders with stylized floral motifs, the overall palette, and the handwritten inscription in French, indicated that the artworks were commissioned by Polier, who had rapidly developed an atelier (design studio) for himself while living in Faizabad. Mihr Chand was the *de facto* Head of this personal atelier, and executed several interesting works while in the employ of Polier. Other craftsmen in his employ were Dulichand, Maulvi Mir Haider Ali and the binder (of the folios), Mir Mohammad Azim. In 1773, Polier had been allotted *Haveli Darab Ali Khan* by Shuja-ud-Daula for his residence (Darab Ali was a courtier in the service of Bahu Begum, chief consort or *Khas Mahal* of Shuja-ud-Daula); the former was dissatisfied with the condition and the Indo-Islamic layout of the building and introduced extensive re-modelling of the structure. Ironically, as Polier was busy with military campaigns during the intervening period, the re-modelling was done by local craftsmen, under the supervision of Martin and Gentil!

In fact, Polier was one of those foreign adventurers in India, who later became "completely native", adopting Indian dress, language and customs. He had become wealthy from his commissions for court buildings as well as from private trading, and he built a residential complex near Lucknow that he called "Polierganj" (in Mohan, present day Unnao district). Polierganj had a spacious bungalow where he maintained his library, botanical and natural history specimens and worked on translations. He studied Hindu mythology and poetry and also engaged in a broad range of commercial activities, which included trading in spices, laying of fruit-bearing gardens, trading in liquor, cloth, and even elephants. Being a prolific writer, he wrote several books on the people and customs of India, and was awarded the title of *Arsalān-i-Jang* by the Mughal court. Polier married twice, both time to Indian ladies and was in close touch with Claude Martin in Lucknow. Later in life, with the immense wealth acquired from his stay in India, he left Indian shores, after leaving his two wives in the care of Martin. However, he did not live long to enjoy the fruits of his foreign adventures. During the violence that had erupted in Europe due to the French Revolution, he was assassinated on February 9, 1795, in the town on Avignon.

Polier was survived by his young Swiss wife, their three children (a daughter and two sons), and his three Indian children. An Indian daughter and son arrived in France together with Polier, and his other son George went to London after his father's death. with another friend of Polier's, Benoît de Boigne, who took responsibility for educating him together with his own Indian children.

Colonel Jean-Baptiste Gentil: Jean-Baptiste Joseph Gentil was born in Bagnols, Languedoc on June 25, 1726; he arrived in Pondicherry in 1752 as an officer of an infantry regiment, to "satisfy his curiosity after learning of the wealth of the Mughal empire." He soon distinguished himself under various French generals *viz.* Joseph Dupleix, Charles Bussy, Jean Law de Lauriston and Comte de Lally being promoted to Lieutenant in 1760 and Captain, ten years later. He saw action and intrigues in Pondicherry, Chandernagore and Murshidabad. Deeply distressed with the decline and fall of French influence in the Indian sub-continent, Gentil made his way to Bengal, to join Mir Qasim in 1761. Later, he migrated to the court of Shuja-ud-Daula, with a following of some two hundred and sixty soldiers, most of them deserters from French and British camps. With time, the number of Frenchmen in Shuja's court increased by leaps and bounds, with Gentil styling himself as the French Resident at Faizabad. 1764 onwards saw the Frenchman literally becoming Shuja's *aide-de-camp* due to his knowledge of Persian language, advising the Nawab on diverse matters, and establishing a battalion of French mercenaries. Gentil's main role veered towards the modernisation and reorganisation of Shuja's infantry and artillery, and the fortification of Faizabad on European principles. This naturally invited the wrath of the British, who started looking upon Gentil as a formidable enemy, bent on fomenting trouble in Awadh. On his part, Gentil made architectural drawings, detailed maps of Mughal India, wrote treatises on historical matters, collected rare / valuable manuscripts and acted on behalf of the Nawab, particularly when negotiating with the British, after the battle of Buxar. His importance can be gauged from the fact that the Mughal Emperor, Shah Alam II, during his visit to Shuja-ud-Daula at Faizabad, paid a personal visit to Gentil at his house.

Shuja-ud-Daula, by overt and covert means, carried out the militarisation of the defeated Awadh army, and for this, he utilised the services of Gentil. An exclusive French corps was constituted, popularly known as *partis francais*. With time, the ranks of this elite corps increased to more than 600, as European soldiers, particularly Frenchmen, made a beeline for Awadh. Gentil functioned as an artillery officer, with an annual salary of 25,000 *rupiya.* High quality firearms were produced in specialised foundries, including muskets and firelocks. As many as 22 foundries and armouries were functional in Awadh during the period. Artificers were employed to manufacture small arms. In the Faizabad foundry, 500 artificers had been employed who produced 150 to 200 firelocks of European design every month. The effectiveness of Awadh firelocks reached its peak when it superseded even the English firelocks in firepower. Unfortunately, all this came to a standstill with the untimely death of Shuja and the disbanding of the *partis francais*. The manufacture of sophisticated weaponry also came to a halt, as Asaf-ud-Daula preferred to depend on the British for supply of firearms.

Thus, we see that if Claude Martin was the most prominent Frenchman in the Nawabi court at Lucknow, Gentil was the most notable Frenchman in the erstwhile Nawabi court of Faizabad. Taking advantage of Shuja-ud-Daula's intense aversion for the British, coupled with humiliating defeats at their hands, Gentil was able to propagate French influence, not only in the Nawab's military establishment, but also other spheres like art and architecture. After his defeat at the battle of Buxar, Shuja's concern was for the safety of his personal effects and family, in the event of any subsequent British attack. The solution was to construct a strong fort at Faizabad, which would be comparable to Fort William, Calcutta. Accordingly, he tried his level best to have it erected, and even gave it a name: *Fort Calcutta* or *Calcutta Khurd*, ironically requesting the British to help him in this venture. The reason for this strange nomenclature of the proposed fort has never been deciphered; perhaps it was done to humour the British and lull them into a false sense of security. The Nawab was convinced that the standard eighteenth century European prototype (*trace italienne*) for a fortress would be most suitable for Awadh. It is significant to note that the Nawabs of Awadh had never built any exclusive fortresses during their regime; those at Chunar and Allahabad, built by the Mughals, were under British control. The *Jalalabad* and *Macchi Bhavan* citadels of Lucknow were of great antiquity. Accordingly, a site plan was proposed on the banks of the river Ghagra (Saryu) river for the proposed fort at Faizabad, but with the British dilly-dallying over its construction, Shuja was left with no other option but to consult the trusted French officers of his court. It was Gentil, who provided the actual architectural layout of the fort, which, by 1773, was speedily built (but not completed) under the supervision of another French officer named M. Canaple, with a work force of thirty to forty thousand workers. The fort walls, although made of mud and *lakhauri* bricks, using wooden supports, were apparently sixty feet thick, the structure having six bastions at intervals. With time, many of Shuja's creations became contiguous, stretching across the city, on the right bank of the river. Western travellers had difficulty in distinguishing between the various palaces and the fortress. Shuja's mother, Nawab Begum and wife, Bahu Begum had continued to live in the premises, even after the death of the Nawab; thereafter it was abandoned, after which it quickly fell into decay when Asaf-ud-Daula shifted his capital from Faizabad to Lucknow. How many of these strong structures became derelict within a short span of time, while others, including the tombs are still extant in Faizabad is a moot question.

The *tripolia* gate has always been a hallmark of the monuments of Awadh; this kind of gateway first appeared in the *Chowk* at Faizabad, and later at *Gulab Bari*. The *tripolia* gate formation in the early phase of Awadh architecture was apparently the creation of Gentil; it would later acquire more elaborate forms under Asaf-ud-Daula and subsequent rulers at Lucknow. The gates were composed of single pointed arches, framed within recessed, foliated ones, surmounted by three smaller arches, and a flat roofline. The central arch was flanked by a trio of three, smaller, superimposed arches. All three smaller side arches (on each side) had different architectural designs, with the bottom one being a blind arch and the others being oriel, curvilinear types, the top one having a bay window, supported by corbels. This basic design was to become a prototype for later Nawabi gateways of Lucknow. Unlike Polier, Gentil was not a qualified engineer or architect. Nevertheless, he had a deep interest in architecture (and archaeology) and prepared several architectural drawings. Although these were often not to scale, and did not follow the canons of draughtsmanship, nevertheless, in present times, they provide useful information on the architectural marvels which had been created for a short while at Faizabad, during the heydays of Nawabi rule, but are no longer extant now. Also, while Asaf-ud-Daula might be credited for raising the status of Lucknow through his architectural creations, it was actually Shuja-ud-Daula and his team of intrepid Frenchmen, particularly Gentil (and Polier), who had actually laid the foundations of Awadh architecture at Faizabad.

Gentil returned to Chandernagore, and by October 1778 was back in France. He had lived for 25 years in India, spending 11 years at the court of Shuja-ud-Daula. He carried from India among other things, an album containing twenty one maps of the Mughal *subas* that he had drawn according to the *Ain-e-Akbari*, which was presented to the King for his royal library. Having lost his military pension, following the disturbances during the French Revolution, he died in poverty on February 15, 1799 at Bagnol. He is known for his works *viz, Memoires sur l'Hndoustan, Histoire des Radjahs de l'Hindoustan* etc.

Walter Reinhardt Sombre was born on January 27, 1723 at Eisenberg in Rhineland-Palatinate, in south-west Germany, presumably in a peasant family. His original name is under some controversy, but it is more or less established that he joined the French army as a cavalryman under the assumed name of Summer. Due to his dark complexion, or possibly because of his grim and sombre visage, he earned the French nickname of *Le Sombre*. Boarding an Indian bound ship, he reached Pondicherry in 1750, but preferred to act as a mercenary, instead of remaining with his compatriots. With time, he migrated to Bengal and worked briefly with the British EIC, he reached Chandernagore (discussed later in this Chapter) where he was appointed as Sergeant of the garrison. After the defeat of the French at the hands of the British, he joined Mir Qasim, the Nawab of Bengal.

Sombre's name was tarnished due to his involvement in the Patna massacre of 1763. Briefly, Mir Qasim, the son-in-law of Mir Jafar (who had been installed as Nawab of Bengal after a series of treacherous moves by the British, resulting in the Battle of Plassey) did not prove to be as pliable to British wanted him to be, and soon fell out of favour. He moved his capital from Murshidabad in Bengal to Monghyr (in present day Bihar), vigorously opposing British economic and trade policies. With matters reaching a flashpoint between the young Nawab and the British, William Ellis, chief of the EIC factory at Patna attacked the city on June 25, 1763 and ransacked it. The city was speedily recovered from British control by Mir Qasim's forces, with Ellis and Carstairs, the military commandant, attempting to retreat to Awadh. The defeated EIC soldiers, including the imprudent Ellis, were taken to Patna and then to Monghyr, with Carstairs succumbing to his injuries.

The British retaliated by reinstating the ageing Mir Jafar to the *masnad* (royal seat) of Bengal as Nawab and declaring war on Mir Qasim, who was then in Patna. When the latter heard that the British had captured the fort of Monghyr, on October 1, 1763, he gave orders that all British prisoners in his custody be put to death. While his other officials were hesitant to carry out mass murder, Reinhardt "Sombre" carried out his orders between October 5 - 11, 1763; Fifty one British personnel, including 16 civilians and thirty five soldiers lost their lives in this incident, including Ellis, who had precipitated this crisis due to his sanguine nature and rash actions. Patna's governor, Raja Ram Narain was also shot down by Sombre on the Nawab's orders.

The circumstances under which Sombre had carried out the killings, however, need to be examined. Sombre had personally confided to Louis Laurent de Féderbe, popularly called Comte de Modave (another French soldier, who had served as Adjutant under de Lally in 1747) that he had tried his outmost to make Mir Qasim desist from his intention; the latter had then threatened Sombre with execution if he did not carry out his orders. Gentil, who was in Awadh corroborated this version of the Patna massacre. In fact, Sombre had become fearful of Mir Qasim's violent temper and impetuosity. Earlier, Mir Qasim had beheaded Gurghis Khan (the *Wolf*, a mercenary soldier of Armenian origin), who was his own military commander, after the British capture of Murshidabad in 1763.

Sombre migrated to Faizabad and joined the forces of Shuja-ud-Daula, who was supporting Mughal Emperor, Shah Alam II and Mir Qasim, making preparations to attack the British. This would end disastrously with the Battle of Buxar in October, 1764. Shuja's infantry was commanded by Gentil, who advised the Nawab of Awadh to go on the offensive against the EIC forces (led by Major Hector Munro, Giles Stibbert, John Carnac and Alexander

Champion), instead of waiting for the British to attack. This advice was apparently disregarded by Shuja. Some authors are of the view that Sombre had not joined Shuja; he was very much with Mir Qasim, commanding a regiment equipped with modern artillery. However, Mir Qasim did not give him the necessary orders to join Shuja at the forefront of the battle with Major John Carnac. And it was only later that Shuja enticed Sombre to formally join him, after the French-German mercenary had looted the treasures of Mir Qasim, everything being fair in love and war.

With the British baying for his blood, Sombre, who was then leading a group of three hundred men of different nationalities, left Awadh and marched to Rajasthan to join the Raja of Bharatpur. With time, he raised his own army, which consisted of four battalions of infantry, one of cavalry and six guns; his officers were solely of European origin. Sombre was now a true mercenary, hiring out his services to any native chief, who could afford him, but he remained faithful to the cause of the Mughal empire. He was awarded a *jagir* by the Mughal court for his services, which later became the Principality of Sardhana (near Meerut). By this time, he had become immensely wealthy, powerful and a close associate of the Mughal emperor. Sombre died in 1778 and was succeeded by his wife, Farzana, popularly known as Begum Sombre or Samru. The Begum was a worthy successor and under her leadership the legacy of Sombre attained greater heights of success and fame. But that is a different story altogether, beyond the scope of this book.

Major General Claude Martin was born on January 5, 1735, to Fleury Martin and Anne Vaginay in the rue de la Palme, Lyons, France. Martin's family background was modest. As a young boy, he studied at the local parish school, where he excelled in mathematics and physics. After leaving school, he was apprenticed to a local silk weaver. At the age of 16, he decided to join the French East India Company to seek his fortunes in India. Martin served under Dupleix and de Lally, but when the French were routed by the British, he offered his services to the English East India Company, which were grudgingly accepted. Martin came in contact with Shuja-ud-Daula and also Asaf-ud-Daula probably in 1774 at Lucknow and he joined the newly appointed Nawab's services in 1776 as Superintendent of his arsenal, duly approved by the Company. He was granted permission by Calcutta to permanently reside at Lucknow, remain exempt from military duties, hold the rank of Major but draw the allowances of a Captain. With the passage of time, he not only managed to ingratiate himself to Asaf-ud-Daula, he also proceeded to engage himself in a number of profitable ventures, which ranged from indigo cultivation to casting cannons. Martin invested his wealth wisely in land and property - and seemingly ended up owning at least eleven houses in Lucknow, in addition to properties in Calcutta and a "palace" in Biposi, Najafgarh - the site of his indigo cultivation venture, on the banks of the Ganga, near Cawnpore (Kanpur). He set up a *Captain Bazar* for providing luxuries and European goods to moneyed buyers (on the south bank of the Gomti, roughly in the area where the Martyr's Memorial stands today). Martin's crowning glory was of course, *Lakhi Pera* or Constantia, which was not completed during his lifetime, and ultimately became his mausoleum. It was never established where he lived during his early years in Lucknow, but he shifted to his "Country House" or *Chateau de Lyon* (later renamed as *Farhat Baksh* by Sa'adat Ali Khan) in 1781.

Fig. 2: Claude Martin's *Chateau de Lyon* at Lucknow, I. Sewell Cornbill (1790).

Martin had the chateau barricaded with a moat, a draw bridge, iron doors, battlements and narrow stairways to provide sufficient security to the residents of the building. With his phenomenal wealth, he experimented with electricity and air pumps to create vacuums; he imported steam engines to pump water in his estate and he studied astronomy from his roof pavilions with a telescope made by William Herschel of the Royal Astronomical Society. It is also conjectured by some writers that the powerful telescope of Martin was used more for surveying the countryside for impending trouble, than for surveying the constellations.

After the death of Martin, the inventory of his estate included an extensive library, scientific equipment, moulds for striking coins and medals, a printing press, an English pipe organ, a billiard table, a suit of armour, a magic lantern, and myriads of other knick-knacks. The chandeliers of the *Farhat Baksh* were purchased from the estate and installed in the Throne Room of Richard Wellesley's New Government House (present *Raj Bhavan*) at Calcutta. The *kothi* was auctioned and bought by Joseph Queiros (Martin's long-time associate) for Rs 40,000, when he outbid Sa'adat Ali Khan, the reigning Nawab of Awadh. Apparently, the Nawab had earlier stayed in the *kothi* for sometime to recuperate from an illness, and had developed an attachment for the same. Therefore, he exerted pressure on Queiros to re-sell the building to him. After Sa'adat Ali Khan took over its ownership, its battlements were removed and its interiors were modified in accordance with the requirements of a palace than a fortress.

It goes to his credit that Martin never took sides; he was on friendly terms with the British, he had many friends among the French and his influence in the Nawabi court at Lucknow was unparalleled. But he also had his fair share of detractors. According to Tribunus (1908), although Martin was "*a gentleman of talents, intelligence, knowledge of the world, of pre-eminent skill and gallantry in his profession, he was unhappily cursed with an irritation and impatience of temper, as galling to others as harassing to himself. He was naturally imperious and opinionated, conceited of his rank, and presumptuous of his descent.*" Col. Jack Warren of the EIC wrote deprecatingly about Martin, as one "*who hung perpetually over the Nawab's seat, smirking benignantly when royalty smirked, and anticipating royalty's every wish. His compatriots seemed to regard him with a mild disgust, though they were careful not to let the Captain himself observe it; since the position he had achieved at this court already rendered him an enemy to be reckoned with, if he were offended.*"

Martin never married, possibly due to a medical condition, as a result of which, he did not have any legal heirs. After his untimely death on September 13, 1800, his enormous fortune and estate

Fig. 3: Constantia and the *Lath* (obelisk), Unidentified Artist, (1820).

remained disputed for several decades, although he had left a detailed, if rather convoluted will. Martin was buried in his new home, *Constantia*, at Lucknow, in which he never had the good fortune to live in. The prestigious La Martiniere schools in Lucknow, Calcutta (Kolkata) and Lyons and several endowments are symbols of his generous legacy. Martin's motto on life was: *Labore et Constantia*, a motto which he constantly adhered to in his lifetime, and which was adopted and shared by the schools bearing his name today.

Lucknow and Chandernagore: Ghiretti House

Presently, Chandernagore (also spelled Chandannagar, Chandernagar and Chandangore) is a small town, located 30 km north of Kolkata, along the banks of Hooghly river. The first factory of the French East India Company had been built here in 1688. Historians are of the opinion that André Bourreau-Deslandes, the French Director General of Commerce in Bengal, had created the actual settlement in 1690, by amalgamating various smaller localities in the area. At some point of time, it was also known as *Faras Danga* (French Land). The connection of the place with sandalwood cannot be ruled out. However, it was not till the Governorship of Dupleix, that the place gained commercial and political importance. Thereafter, it prospered as a French colony, till Admiral Watson bombarded it in 1757, due to hostilities breaking out between England and France in Europe. Clive ordered its fortifications to be pulled down, in retaliation for the conduct of Count Lally in Madras. It was restored to the French in 1765 in a ruinous condition; the old *Fort d'Orléans* has been pulled down; the larger buildings were in a dilapidated condition and its population had dwindled. Chandernagore's (mis)fortunes waivered frequently over the next century, and by 1900, it had become a ghost town. Today, it survives as a satellite town of Kolkata, with some colonial edifices still worth visiting.

During his tenure at Chandernagore as Governor (1767 - 1778), Jean-Baptiste Chevalier had closely watched the developments at Awadh, and had been keen to establish official contact with the *suba*. Chevalier was an enterprising and patriotic Bengal veteran who in the 1750s had led a series of expeditions to establish trading links with the kingdom of Assam. Chevalier was a charismatic persona, who believed that even after 1765, it was possible for France to create a sphere of influence in the Indian sub-continent. He was aware that Shuja-ud-Daula was smarting under ignominious defeat at the hands of the British in Battle of Buxar (1764), and hence was open to alliances against them. Chevalier was convinced that the Nawab Wazir was favourably inclined towards the French, and was the only powerful ruler in north India, who would be willing to thwart the British on an opportune moment. Later, however, after the ascension of Asaf-ud-Daula, Chevalier shifted his attentions to wooing the Mughals and Marathas on a similar mission, i.e. to somehow put a hold on Britain's increasing military successes.

Nawab Shuja-ud-Daula of Awadh had some reservations in anointing his eldest son, Asaf-ud-Daula as his successor (details of which are beyond the scope of this discussion). However, Bahu Begum, his principal and famous consort prevailed upon him, and Shuja-ud-Daula's choice, Sa'adat Ali Khan (son from another begum) was sidelined. When Asaf-ud-Daula took over the reigns of Awadh in 1775, he shifted his capital from Faizabad to Lucknow to avoid conflict with his mother, Bahu Begum. He also perceived a threat from Sa'adat Ali, and ordered the latter to present himself, with his troops at Lucknow. Sa'adat Ali preferred to stay away from his half brother (due to obvious reasons) and spent much of his youth as a sort of exile, at Benaras, Calcutta and Chandernagore.

Fig. 4: Aquatint of Ghiretti House, Chandernagore, James Moffat (1800).

Sa'adat Ali was exposed to western influences from his youth. He was impressed by colonial architecture and town planning, and while at Chandernagore, he stayed at a chateau called Ghiretti House (Ghiretta House), which was the French Governor's residence (and not the one called Dupleix's Palace, situated at Strand Road, Chandernagore). Ghiretti House was so named because it was situated at Gourhati or Goretty, south of Chandernagore proper.

It was separated from Chandernagore by a small strip of land or corridor under British control. The residence was reported to have been built by Dupleix and lavishly furnished by Chevalier. With its elegant staircases, saloons, and painted ceilings, the chateau of Ghiretty was thought by some to rival the palace of Versailles in splendour. Fortunately, under Chevalier's Governorship, signs of prosperity had begun to return to Chandernagore and the fortunes of Ghiretti House kept changing as Chandernagore changed hands from French to British ownership several times. Ironically, Chevalier enjoyed close personal relationship with British officials of Calcutta, many of whom visited the chateau on weekends as official guests of the French officer. During the times of British occupation or control, Ghiretti House was occupied by several British officials also, including Sir Eyre Coote, during the heydays of the conflict between Hastings, Philip Francis and the rest. It was also inhabited by the European garrison for sometime. The last vestiges of the palace was described by Firminger (*Bengal, Past and Present*, Vol. II, 1908) as well as Bishop Heber in his journals:

Dead Ghyretty's pictured ceiling
Sleeps beneath the jungle shade
By the serpent-track revealing
Cornice-wreck and balustrade
And the ghosts go ever stealing
Down the wind-bit esplanade...

To come back to Sa'adat Ali, he continued to absorb European life styles; he was also reportedly tutored by Mlle. Galliex from Chandernagore, which further developed his eclectic tastes. When the British anointed him as Nawab of Awadh in 1798, he gave full vent to his feelings and re-modelled Lucknow, by cutting a straight road across the city and building several beautiful buildings in his capital. He bought Claude Martin's house, *Lakhi Pera*, and remodelled it as his residence, *Farhat Baksh*. He was responsible for building the *Dilkusha Kothi*, which was modelled on a manor called Seaton Delavel in Northumberland, UK. For his favourite begum, Khurshid Zadi, he had the *Khurshid Manzil* built, which resembled an English castle, complete with turrets and a moat. The imposing *Musa Bagh Kothi* or *Barowen* in *Musa Bagh* was designed by the Nawab himself.

Apparently, the northern facade of *Barowen* was inspired by the south-side portico of Government House in Calcutta, which itself was based on Kedleston Hall, an English country house in Kedleston, Derbyshire, built earlier in 1759. Sa'adat Ali's contributions to Lucknow's development are too numerous to be described in detail in this Chapter.

Fig. 5: Tablet in Sacred Heart Church, Chandernagore, PC Sarkar (2018).

Back in Chandernagore, Ghiretti House had a less fortunate end. The building was eventually pulled down and a jute mill, Angus Jute Works was built on its grounds. The mill was in the news in the recent past due to less pleasant reasons. It was owned by M/s Thomas Duff & Co, an old Scottish, Dundee - based company, incorporated in 1883.

At present, there is no trace of the former residence of the French Governor in the area (Bhadreshwar), where British General, Sir Eyre Coote "loitered with his wife, fit for nothing else."

So was Sa'adat Ali the only connection between Lucknow and Chandernagore? Not quite. Claude Martin, the maverick French soldier who served under Comte de Lally at Pondicherry, and later offered his services to the British, left considerable endowments for the poor (irrespective of religion) in Lyon (his home town in France), Lucknow, Calcutta and Chandernagore. He also left instructions for tablets to be affixed, for "commemorating his benefactions and explain his purposes." The author came across this tablet affixed at the entrance of Sacred Heart Church, Chandernagore, which essentially states that Maj Gen. Claude Martin had left an endowment of Rs 50,000, the interest from which, was to be distributed daily among the poor of Chandernagore for perpetuity. Till the writing of this book, it could not be ascertained if the poor of Chandernagore still benefit from this endowment fund set up by Martin.

Antoine De L'Etang was another French maverick soldier in the Awadh court, whom we shall now discuss. Born in Versailles, France on July 20, 1757, his first appointment was in the Palace of Versailles, as a Page of Honour to princess Maria Antonia, who would later become famous in history as Marie Antoinette, the last queen of France. It has been alleged that the two fell in love with each other, which caused his expulsion from the French court by royal decree and being exiled to India in 1784. By this time, he had gained sufficient experience in the breeding and upkeep of horses, as he had been the Superintendent of the Royal Stud Farm, before his exile. It is also possible that he might have left French shores on his own, fearing imprisonment, because of his clandestine affair. His experience with *farriery* (equine hoof care) stood him in good stead, when he chose to quit the service of the French and reach Calcutta, to set up stables and a school for horse riding in partnership with another Frenchman named Julius Soubise. He also dabbled in the auctioning of horses and their veterinary care. In 1802, De L'Etang was appointed as a veterinary surgeon to the Bodyguard (a cavalry regiment) of Lord Wellesley, then Governor General of Bengal. But his good fortunes did not last long due to a series of unfortunate events, including an epidemic, which caused many of the horses in the Bodyguard to fall ill and die.

To seek his fortunes once again, De L'Etang reached the court of Awadh at Lucknow and joined the services of Sa'adat Ali Khan, as Superintendent of the Nawab's stables and Veterinary Surgeon. Sa'adat Ali Khan had built the magnificent *Chaupar Astabal* or Cruciform Stables for his horses and had been on the lookout for a suitable candidate to supervise and maintain his stables, which was an immense structure based on the Panopticon model. Unfortunately, misfortune continued to dog the Frenchman, as he faced resistance from other native officials in the Nawabi court; the death of several prize horses in the stables was attributed to his incompetence as a veterinarian, and he found no support from Sa'adat Ali's son and successor, Ghazi-ud-Din Haider (who would later assume the title of the first king of Awadh). Eventually, De L'Etang was dismissed from the new Nawab's services, along with several other Europeans loyal to the former Nawab Sa'adat Ali Khan (including Capt. Duncan McLeod, credited for designing the *Khurshid Manzil* palace at Lucknow and *Hazarduari* palace or *Nizamat Qila* at Murshidabad). However, De L'Etang was speedily reinstated at Calcutta as Sub-Assistant to the Superintendent of the EIC stables (stud). He died in Buxar on December 1, 1840.

Chapter - IV

Of Valour and Fortitude

> *We were continually insulted by the music of the mutineers. At early dawn their bugles regularly began sounding the assembly, and a variety of regimental calls; while the shrill horns and drums of the Rujwarra (a name used to designate the zemindarree* (sic) *forces) kept up loud and dissonant screams. which were again renewed every evening. Occasionally their bands paraded in our sight and played "God save the Queen," or other tunes which they had learnt in our service.*
>
> **- Martin Gubbins,**
> Financial Commissioner, Lucknow Residency (1857)

Historical Background

Lucknow's tryst with the tragic events of 1857 started on May 2, 1857, when the 4th and 7th Oudh Irregular Infantry stationed at *Musa Bagh* in the outskirts of the city refused to bite the greased cartridges, almost a week ahead of the uprising in Meerut on May 10, 1857 (officially accepted as the commencement of India's First War of Independence). The rebellion quickly spread to the British cantonment at *Madiaon* on the north end of Lucknow city, across the river. Almost a year later, it was the turn of Ahmadullah 'Danka' Shah, and then Begum Hazrat Mahal, to take refuge in *Musa Bagh*. Outram advanced towards the *kothi* on March 19, 1858, with a formidable force. However, even after a fierce fight, the British were unable to capture the *begum*, who left for Nepal, following a circuitous route through the hinterlands of Awadh, personally camping in the estates of many of the local *rajas*, exhorting them to fight for the liberation of Awadh from Company rule.

Between May 1857 and March 1858, Lucknow and its environs saw a number of battles between the Indian freedom fighters and

British soldiers. Lucknow's soldiers or *sepoys* did not march in formations, under pennants, accompanied by the blowing of bugles. After the annexation of Awadh, many of the Indian soldiers had not received their paltry salaries - several having been dismissed from the ex-King's service, but not re-appointed in the EIC. The freedom-fighters did not have a unified leadership, nor did they possess modern firepower and logistic support by semaphore, and yet they fought with valour and fortitude. The reason for this was that they were battling, not for commercial considerations or for loot, but for their motherland from where they had been summarily dispossessed; they were fighting with their backs against the wall, against tremendous odds, accepting the bitter truth that there would be no quarter - that the final outcome would either be liberation or death. Even for the common citizens of Lucknow, it was a struggle for a religious cause and more importantly, for self-respect. They fondly remembered the good old times under a benevolent ruler, who had been an accomplished litterateur and danseuse - a person who had ruled by affection rather than through awe and fear. Subsequent historical findings would prove that almost no class of Lucknow's populace had remained unrepresented and that people from all walks of life, caste and creed had been steadfast in their struggle for freedom from a foreign government.

The re-capture of Lucknow by British forces is often demarcated into *First Relief* led by Havelock and Outram and subsequent *Second Relief* commanded by Colin Campbell. This demarcation is a misnomer, since the campaign led Outram could offer no relief to the besieged in the Residency. At best, the disastrous outcome Outram's campaign and his personal knowledge of Lucknow's terrain was utilised by Campbell, who avoided committing the same blunder as Outram. We shall now deliberate on these battles of Lucknow, without any bias or prejudice - more as a tribute, if nothing else; as an acknowledgment of the sacrifices of thousands of Indian freedom fighters, whose remains still lie in nameless graves and mounds in and around the city of Lucknow.

And So It Began: The Battle of *Chinhat*

Lucknow's urban growth in the last decade has subsumed a rural area called *Chinhat*, which was described in old British *Gazetteers* as a "*village lying on the metalled road from Lucknow to Fyzabad, at a distance of about six miles from the former.*" The name *Chinhat* was possibly derived from the term, *Chana Haat* or gram market, which had flourished in the area from the times of Ghazi-ud-Din Haider. The battle which took place here (more specifically near Ismailganj, a sub-locality in present day Indiranagar) between the British and Indian freedom fighters on June 30, 1857 has several versions. It had been a significant engagement since it had resulted in the complete routing of British forces, which had limped back to the Residency in tatters. Naturally the EIC tried to downplay the battle and its outcome, displaying a wilful amnesia. Martin Gubbins, who had been the Financial Commissioner brought out his own version of the battle, which obliquely blamed Henry Lawrence, the Chief Commissioner, for the debacle. Gubbins was a civilian, who also had a record of confrontation with Coverley Jackson, the predecessor of Lawrence. Although Gubbins' version found few takers and his reputation was damaged, yet, it formed a valuable source of alternate history, different from the "official" version.

Briefly, on June 29, a spy had informed Lawrence that an Indian contingent, composed of *Tilangas* (Indian soldiers trained by the British), *Risala* (irregular cavalry) and two cannons had reached Aliganj (then on the outskirts of Lucknow), and that a 7000 - 15000 strong army of rebel forces was likely to join them shortly. Lawrence decided to engage the approaching rebel army on the outskirts of Lucknow, before they entered the city proper. Accordingly, in the morning of June 30, 1857, he set off with a force composed of European and Indian soldiers, equipped with adequate firepower, with the intention of checking their approach. The British army consisted of 300 Sikh soldiers loyal to the British, 80 horsemen, 1200 *barqandaz* (soldiers armed with a matchlocks), 5 companies of *Tilangas*, 11 companies of British soldiers, 50 heavy pieces of artillery driven by horses and bullocks, including a howitzer, drawn by an elephant, which started from the Residency before dawn. Actually, the composition of Lawrence's force has been hotly debated and the numbers indicated above are not unequivocal. Another source quotes the total number of men to be merely 496, with 9 pieces of artillery, including the 8 inch howitzer. Nearing the Kukrail (a tributary of the Gomti) river, the Company forces could not discern the revolutionaries, who were well concealed in the marshes and behind trees. Simultaneously, several Indian soldiers accompanying the forces of Lawrence deserted and joined their compatriots. The rebels also overturned the heavy British guns into ditches, where they got stuck and proved to be useless; these could not even be dragged back or recovered. The revolutionaries then fired upon the European forces from three sides, forcing the latter to retreat, with heavy casualties. In the general mêlée and panic, the heavy pieces of artillery were left behind, which were promptly appropriated by the Indian forces. The freedom fighters pursued the British forces, who beat a hasty retreat back into the city, till the pursuers faced shelling from *Macchi Bhavan* and Baillie Guard gate of the Residency. The siege of Lucknow's Residency commenced forthwith.

According to Gubbins, his intelligence network had informed about the movement of revolutionaries near Bara Banki (a mofussil town in the outskirts of Lucknow), which he had duly communicated to Lawrence, who set off the next day to engage with the enemy. But the movement of British troops had started too late; the sun was up and the heat excessive. They had been surrounded by the revolutionaries and the Sikh horsemen, accompanied by native artillery, could offer no support to Lawrence from the blistering attack of the Indian soldiers, who had concealed themselves behind mangroves on either side of the road. The banks of the road were steep, as a result of which the heavy guns overturned into the ditch. The British officers and men faced a volley of fire, and many were mortally wounded; the Sikh soldiers behaved shamefully and fled. A retreat was now ordered but the restless animals hauling the howitzers panicked and many of the guns had to be abandoned as the artillery drivers detached the horses from the guns and ammunition wagons before fleeing. The British defeat was accompanied by the loss of an eight-inch howitzer, all the ammunition wagons, with at least 112 soldiers being killed and 44 injured. It had been a sad day for the British but an occasion of rejoicing among the native population, including civilians.

Indian sources, mostly based on oral tradition are more forthwith. Due to fear of reprisals by the victorious British, written records had not been maintained by the Indian side. Whatever documents were available too were destroyed by the local populace for the same reason.

In fact, the events at Chinhat / Ismailganj had been preceded by Raja Nawab Ali of Mahmudabad assuming leadership of the Awadh forces, under the military command of Khan Ali Khan (former *chakladar* of Salon, a *pargana* in present-day Rae Bareilly district, who had been earlier dismissed from his services at the instance of Col. Sleeman), together with Barqat Ahmad as General and Ahmadullah "Danka" Shah as Commander. Other Indian freedom fighters to hold important military ranks were Hisam-ud-Daula, Saugan Singh, Sarjoo Singh, Bahadur Ali and Yusuf Khan. Raja Jai Lal Singh, former *nazim* of Azamgarh was the spokesperson for the Indian soldiers. He was an adept in guerrilla warfare tactics. Sayyid Barqat Ahmad was a former *risaldar* of the 15th Bengal Irregular Cavalry, whose role in the events of 1857 is largely forgotten. Maulvi Ahmadullah Shah was not a trained soldier, yet as a commander, he displayed great ability in tactical warfare. He was a born leader of men and a fearless warrior for the "cause." "Danka" Shah's further forays against the British shall be described later in this Chapter, being the only revolutionary leader to have twice defeated Colin Campbell. The advancing Indian forces was composed of several *paltans* (platoons). These included the 2nd Native Infantry from Faizabad (which had originally mutinied in Barrackpore, Bengal, Oude as well as Infantry Oude Irregular Forces from Secrora (Sikrora), Durriabad (Daryabad), Gonda, Sitapur and Sultanpur, among others. Although the *ta'aluqdars* (landed barons) had joined the revolutionaries, they did not join the battle, but were kept on reserve. The native troops under the command of Subedar Ghamandi Singh and Subedar Shahabuddin also fought bravely, joined by Afridi warriors from Malihabad.

Without first sending a reconnoitring party and sensing an easy victory, Lawrence, had directly led his forces from Lucknow towards Chinhat to confront the revolutionaries. It has been alleged that Lawrence was so sure of victory that he had proceeded on a *buggy* (horse-drawn carriage) instead of horseback. His miscalculation proved to be catastrophic for the British. Under a volley of fire from three sides, the British forces had tried to retreat inside Ismailganj, but were driven out, being outflanked by the revolutionaries; the former had no choice but to flee to the Residency, after a pitched battle at Kukrail bridge. The British were pursued by the Indian freedom fighters till the Iron Bridge inside the city, where a heavy engagement again took place. The defeated army ultimately reached the safety of the Residency under a cover of fire from *Macchi Bhavan* and the Baillie Guard gate. After the bloody battle at Chinhat / Ismailganj was over, only 11 Indian soldiers had been martyred and "Danka" Shah wounded in the foot. The British losses included nearly 200 casualties, 44 wounded and the loss of artillery and ammunition, including an eight-inch howitzer. During the battle, flags depicting both Hindu and Islamic religious symbols, together with battle cries of *Jai Bajrang Bali, Ya Ali* and *Ek Pita Do Santaan, Ek Hindu Do Musalman* had rent the air, indicating complete Hindu-Muslim amity among the freedom fighters. The outcome of the Battle of Chinhat had been devastating for the British forces and a reason for high morale among the Awadh forces and local populace. However, as subsequent events would unfold, the fervour and good fortune would not sustain long for the Indian side.

The Battle(s) of Bashiratganj

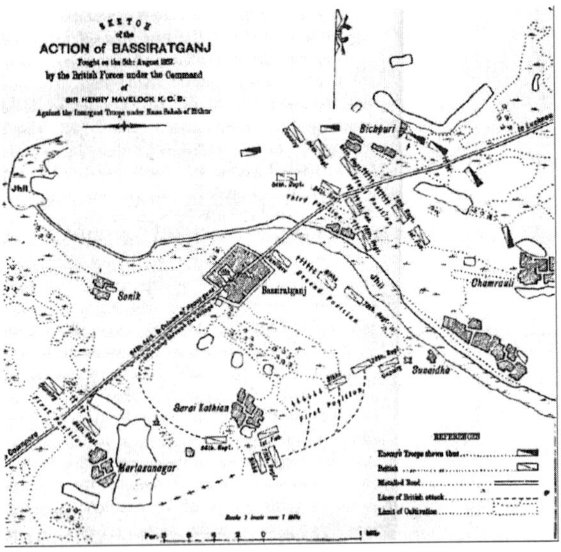

Fig. 6: Old British Map depicting action at Bashiratganj (1857).

Bashiratganj or "Busherutgunge / Bassiratganj" of 1857 has been described in old colonial records as "*a walled town beyond Onao*

(Unnao) *towards Lucknow, with wet ditches, having a gate defended by a round tower, four pieces of cannon on and near the tower, loop holed and strengthened buildings within the walls, and a broad and deep lake beyond the town*." The place was a sort of "chicken neck", through which passage was inevitable, if one approached Lucknow from Cawnpore (Kanpur) using the old Nawabi metalled road, built by Wajid Ali Shah. This road had been of considerable commercial importance during Nawabi times, embellished as it was by spacious *serais* (rest-houses), markets, "handsome" bridges and wells, built by the wealthy of Lucknow to perpetuate their memory. The swamp on one side prevented movement and offered no shelter. The garden enclosure "had purposely or accidentally assumed the form of a bastion" which was a safe haven for the Indian soldiers, who rained "a destructive fire" on the approaching British soldiers. Bashiratganj and its nearby village, Mangalwar or "Mungulwar", was the site of three furious, free-for-all battles, which we shall now discuss in some detail.

Henry Havelock's military prowess had impressed the British government, which resulted in his being sent to Awadh, which was then in the throes of the revolutionary movement. He had been preceded by Col. James Neil, who had laid waste the city and countryside of Allahabad and was on the way to Cawnpore to help the entrenched General Hugh Wheeler. Havelock did not quite agree with the cruel and inhuman ways of Neil, and the two were often at logger-heads over the chain of command, but those were times of war; the British were desperate to wrest back Awadh, which was under the control of the Indian revolutionaries, and the British Residency was under siege at Lucknow. Henry Lawrence at Lucknow congratulated and welcomed Havelock on his arrival at Allahabad on June 27; on that fateful day, General Wheeler's forces had surrendered to Nana Sahib at Cawnpore in return for a safe passage to Allahabad; three days later, it would be the turn of Lawrence to be routed at Chinhat.

Another description of Bashiratganj is as follows:

"It was a walled town, intersected by the high-road to Lucknow. In the rear of it lay a jheel, or sheet of water, about 150 yards in width, and six or seven feet deep, over which the road was carried by a causeway. The main gate, at the hither entrance of the town, was

defended by an earthwork, a trench, and four guns, and flanked on either side by turrets, which were loop holed, as were also the walls. The gate was likewise completely covered by a large building within the town."

After decisive victories in Futteygurh (Fatehgarh), Cawnpore, and Bithoor, it was but natural that Havelock should next concentrate on his original mission, *i.e.* the liberation of Lucknow. He realised that Bashiratganj was a formidable position. The Indian revolutionaries, under the command of Yusuf Khan had not been idle. Any frontal assault would have been suicidal. On July 29, Havelock diverted the 64th Highlanders to march around Bashiratganj to the left and interpose itself between the gate and the causeway. Three guns, posted on the high road were brought to bear on the earthwork and the gateway in front, while a converging fire was directed on the same point from the left and right. The 78th Highlanders and Madras Fusiliers would attempt to storm the gateway, with backup from the 84th and the Sikhs. As the Highlanders and the Fusiliers advanced, they faced a heavy barrage of fire from the Indian revolutionaries. The 64th, instead of advancing, paused to engage and return the fire from the walls; it failed to reach the appointed destination. Havelock sent his aide-de-camp at full gallop to hasten its advance, but the opportunity was lost, and could not be covered.

With the exception of three hours given to rest and refreshments, the British troops had been incessantly marching and fighting from dawn till dusk. As night was approaching, Havelock personally rode for a considerable distance, in search for a suitable position for the night halt of his weary troops. Ultimately, his forces settled for the night, between the *jheel* and the town.

The next day brought no good tidings for the British. A huge band of revolutionaries had been observed hovering nearby, although they did not take any part in the action; these Indian soldiers were reportedly loyal to Nana Sahib and were waiting for his orders. Havelock was also running low on ammunition and supplies and 88 British soldiers had killed with 112 wounded on the previous day. Others were disabled by fatigue, exposure and cholera. It was impossible for him to advance towards Lucknow, unless the wounded and the sick were abandoned, which was unthinkable. In such desperate circumstances, instead of proceeding towards Lucknow, Havelock prudently decided to retreat to Mangalwar village, which was "situated six miles from the river, on a ridge, extending five miles, and elevated about 200 feet above the surrounding country." Due to its elevation, the occupation of this village had strategic importance for the British. The first battle of Bashiratganj had been auspicious for the Indian freedom fighters. More action was yet to come. That the revolutionaries were brave and fearless, even in the face of impending death can be gauged from the following gruesome description (Headley, 1861):

"During the forenoon some prisoners who had been taken and court-martialled, suffered the penalty that was inflicted throughout India on the mutineers. Two were hung on the limb of a tree, while two others found more guilty were sentenced to be blown from the guns. These, stripped naked, were brought out and placed in sight of the suspended corpses. They were splendidly formed men, tall, powerful, and with limbs that seemed modelled from some antique statue. Both were in the prime of life, yet met this horrible death with the same composure they would have lain down to repose. With graceful and dignified step, and head erect, and fearless look, the first walked steadily up to the loaded cannon, and leaned carelessly on the muzzle. Not a quiver of the lip, not a change in the expression of the eye, or hue of the cheek was visible, although the sepoys that looked on were as pale as ashes. When the soldiers had finished binding him, they stepped back, and the word "Fire," broke the breathless silence. A sudden flash, a muffled report, "a sickening effluvia that tainted the atmosphere," - mangled, bleeding and burnt masses of flesh scattered in every direction - the head shooting like a rocket into the sky, and all was over. Nothing daunted, the second met with the same unflinching eye and scornful look the same dreadful fate".

Another narration of this brutal British practice (Fitchett, 1902) goes as follows:

"(On Havelock's orders) *when we halted for the night, I moved one of my guns on to the causeway, unlimbered it, and brought it into "action front." The evening was just beginning to grow dusk, and the enemy were still in sight, on the crest of some rising ground a few hundred yards distant. The remainder of my guns were "parked" in a nice mango tope to the right of the road. The first man led out was a fine looking young sepoy, with good features and a bold, resolute expression. He begged that he might not be bound, but this could not be allowed, and I had his wrists tied tightly each to the upper part of a wheel of the gun. Then I depressed the muzzle, until it pointed to the pit of his stomach, just below the sternum. We put no shot in and I only kept one gunner (besides the firing number) near the gun. standing myself about 10 ft. to the left rear. The young sepoy looked undauntedly at us during the whole process of pinioning; indeed he never flinched for a moment. Then I ordered the port-fire to be lighted and gave the word "Fire!" There was a considerable recoil from the gun and a thick cloud of smoke hung over us. As this cleared away we saw two legs lying in front of the gun but no other sign of what had, just before, been a human being and a brave man. At this moment, perhaps six to eight seconds after the explosion, down fell the man's head among us, slightly blackened but otherwise scarcely changed. It must have gone straight up into the air probably 200 feet."*

That the British (an epitome of civilisation) "relieving" forces had ample experience in committing mass murders of prisoners of war (referred to as "enemies", "pandies" and other derogatory terms like "niggers" and "beggars") can be gleaned from another earlier reference (August 4, 1857), this time at Peshawar (Maude, 1894):

"Some 200 prisoners of the 55th Regiment, BNI have been tried here (Peshawar) and we blew 40 of them away from our guns, in the presence of the whole Force, three days ago; a fearful but necessary example, which struck terror into their souls. Three sides of a square were formed, ten guns pointed outwards, the sentence of the Court was read, a prisoner bound to each gun, the signal given, and the salvo fired. Such a scene I hope never again to witness - human trunks, legs, arms etc flying about in all directions. All met their fate with firmness, but two, who would not be tied up; so, to save time, they were dropped to the ground, and their brains blown out by musketry."

As is evident from the above graphic descriptions (which are not from Indian sources), the British, including the Bible-bearing Havelock - the latter having a penchant for spewing platitudes and delivering emotional pep talks, could be as inhuman and as murderous as the infamous Neil. Both officers and others of their ilk (like Hodson) had indulged in unnecessary bloodshed and wanton killings during the course of their extended careers as British "soldiers." Ironically, the culmination of their blood-spattered military service was destined to be at Lucknow. After all, fate had to intervene eventually.

Havelock messaged Neil at Cawnpore, requesting another battery and "a thousand British bayonets" before he could advance to Lucknow. However, an open rebellion had broken out at Dinapore (an old British garrison town now called Danapur) near Patna on July 25, and the European troops who would have otherwise proceeded to reinforce Havelock were held back to counter this new band of Native Corps, now on a rampage. Havelock received 257 soldiers from Cawnpore, to augment his force, which was barely sufficient to fill up the casualties he had faced in his earlier battles at Unnao and Bashiratganj. Also, among these 257, there were native Gun Lascars (artillery men, the term derived from the *Farsi* word *lashkar,* meaning military force), who exhibited rebellious tendency. He upbraided them, had them disarmed and sent back to Cawnpore.

The evening of August 4 saw Havelock leaving his encampment at Mangalwar and reaching Unnao, where he camped for the night. Next day, Havelock's force approached Bashiratganj once again, but was halted on reports on the movements of Indian revolutionaries, received from the Voluntary Cavalry which led the advance. Havelock decided to send detachments to sweep round the town, and take up position behind it, between the farther gate and the causeway. Havelock's guns were pushed along the road, brought within three hundred yards of the gate and commenced fire, so that shots and shells swept through the town and exploded. He avoided a frontal man-to-man assault on the town, since he did not want to expose his infantry to the revolutionaries' return fire. Unexpectedly, a heavy cannonade by the revolutionaries commenced from a nearby village, which proved to be a severe impediment for Havelock's progress. Also, he had no cavalry as compared to the Indian side, the latter capturing a British gun and carrying it off with them. Evening fell, but no decisive victory was in sight for the British forces. Havelock's scouts reported that the position at Nawabganj was as strong as that at Bashiratganj, the entire line of road to Lucknow dotted with posts equally difficult. Also the bridge over the Sai river had been broken up by the rebels and the passage of the river heavily guarded by a large force and heavy artillery.

Havelock was aware that every village on the way to Lucknow was opposed to the British, including the landowners, who had suffered in one way or the other after the annexation. In the rear, Nana Sahib was still a formidable force and the Gwalior Contingent was likely to support him. The Dinapore mutineers were advancing rapidly towards Mirzapur, to ultimately join Nana's forces. In such a gloomy scenario for the British, Bashiratganj could be re-occupied anytime, by the Indian rebels. The General prudently decided that instead of holding on to Bashiratganj with his fledgling force, it would be advisable to re-trace his steps once again to Mangalwar. This would be the second feather in the cap of the Indians revolutionaries at Bashiratganj, who speedily re-occupied the town once again, and moved down to Unnao, only a few miles from Havelock's camp. so to be ready to fall upon his troops, the moment they engaged in fording of the river.

The wily General had finally decided to cross the river, and at an unearthly hour of 3.00 am, had the bugles sounded for readying his weary troops for the final assault on Bashiratganj. It was August 12, 1857. The Indian freedom fighters, about 4000 in numbers, including 500 cavalry, had entrenched themselves, not in Bashiratganj but in a village called *Burhia Chowki* near Unnao. A large swamp lay right in front of this position, on which were placed six field guns. Avoiding a frontal attack by crossing the swamp, the British soldiers would approach the Indian position from the left and right sides. The Indian side opened up a furious fusillade, but Havelock trudged on, and getting his guns in position fired heavily on the whole rebel line. The Indian revolutionaries bravely defended their position, but sensing defeat, chose to retreat. The British cavalry could not follow the rebel soldiers through the swamps, and the infantry was too tired to pursue, so a halt was sounded by the blowing of bugles. Due to the element of surprise and dogged determination, the British won the third battle of Bashiratganj, losing merely 35 soldiers in this engagement. The losses on the Indian side was estimated to be around 200. The victory for the British side paved the way for their march to Lucknow, their ultimate destination.

On August 13, 1857, Colin Campbell arrived at Calcutta to assume the office of Commander-in-Chief of the British Indian army. Havelock had been superseded in command by James Outram, the latter reaching Kanpur on September 15. This had been caused due to a number of factors, least of which was Havelock's recommendation of his own son for award of the VC, and his vacillating tactics at Bashiratganj.

The Battles at *Alambagh*

Alambagh was an extensive, fortified palace-cum-garden complex, enclosed by buttressed walls, nine feet high, having bastions at the four corners. A British plan of 1857, showing the fortification of the garden shows a square, with each wall measuring 400 yards (1200 feet). That means the area of the garden complex was 1,440,000 square feet or about 33 acres. The palace itself was right at the centre of the garden with a single entrance through an impressive European-style gateway, bearing the usual fish symbol on its spandrels. It was named after Alam Ara Begum, the *Khas Mahal* (senior-most queen and mother of the crown prince or heir-apparent) of Wajid Ali Shah, who had preferred to reside in her own palace, away from her husband, the King. The *Alambagh Kothi* was situated in the center of the garden, having the usual hybrid architecture of Lucknow's Nawabi era. Described as a "manor-like, windowless building" by the British, the building sported a prominent triangular pediment and octagonal turrets at its four corners. Alam Ala Begum had accompanied Wajid Ali Shah to Calcutta; fate would make her palace complex a beehive of activity during 1857 - initially being occupied by the revolutionaries and later by the British.

September 16 saw Outram waiving his rank and command in favour of Havelock, which he would resume after the relief of Lucknow, as a measure of respect and regard for a fellow officer. This was followed by the re-establishing of the floating bridges, which had been earlier ravaged by the revolutionaries. The British soldiers armed with heavy artillery crossed over with little resistance from the rebel's side, who were in control of Mangalwar. The British troops settled for the night at Bashiratganj and reached the outskirts of *Alambagh* on September 23. The Nawabi garden and its environs

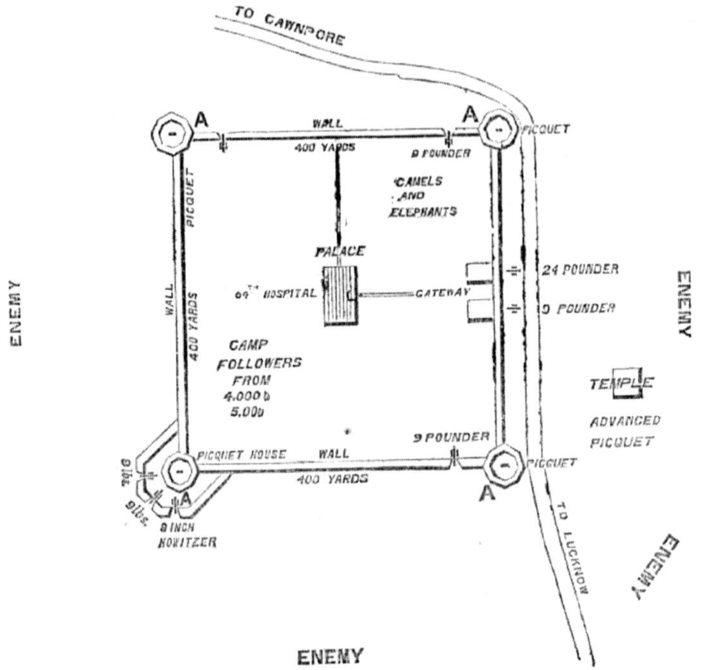

Fig. 7: British fortification at *Alambagh* (1857).

had been heavily fortified by the revolutionaries, forcing the British to stop their advance and go on a reconnoitring mission. It was observed that the former were not only secure in the premises, they were also posted on some mounds nearby. *"This tranquil and lovely aspect formed a singular contrast to the fierce warfare of which it was now to be the scene.*" The freedom fighters' line extended to nearly two miles, supposedly consisting of 10,000 men, while another body of cavalry, estimated at 1500 was amassed on the right, behind marshes and trees. The Indian soldiers had remained silent during the reconnaissance, but as the British column advanced, they faced a withering fire from the former, which caused havoc in the ranks. The Indian side was led by stalwarts such as Rana Beni Madho (of Shankarpur estate in modern-day Rae Bareilly and part of the old Baiswara region in Awadh), Jai Lal of Atraulia (presently Atraulia is a town and a *Nagar Panchayat* in Azamgarh district),

Mirza Baqar Ali and Hira Lal (of Baiswara). With the aid of cavalry, the British managed to silence the guns of the rebels to some extent, although they continued to face a "galling fire" from another of the rebels' position, forcing a retreat. Embrasures had been made through the walls of the garden, which was utilised by the Indian side to fire a volley of shots on the Europeans. However, the tide soon turned, forcing a body of rebels to retreat from their positions. They were pursued till the *Charbagh* bridge by Outram, after which he retreated prudently.

As dawn broke on the next day, the elevation or the ridge where the British soldiers had retired for the night became visible; it was soon bombarded heavily by the rebel soldiers, causing heavy damage to the former. Eight men of the 78th Highlanders were wounded, forcing the British to retreat to a more secure line, away from the rebel's fire. The baggage train containing the provisions of the Europeans had been lagging behind the march; the train extending for more than a mile now reached the *Alambagh,* were suddenly attacked from the rear by the rebels' forces. Some confusion prevented them from responding to the rebel's firing, which caused further casualties among the rear British guard, which included a British officer and several soldiers.

Throughout the day, the rebel soldiers continued to hover around the British encampment, displaying a green flag as a sign of defiance (the *Safavid* dynasty (1501–1736) of Persia had employed various *alams* (flagpoles in Islamic culture, typically surmounted by an ornate metal finial and banners, with different emblems) on a green background). The British campsite was also challenged by two nine-pounders, hidden behind the *Charbagh* bridge, incessantly pounding British positions and causing many casualties.

After Havelock's failed attempt to relieve Lucknow, *Alambagh* was to be the scene for further action. The sick and wounded among the British, together with tents and spare stores had been left at *Alambagh*, in charge of a small detachment. Colin Campbell, the Commander-in-Chief left Cawnpore on November 9 and proceeded to Lucknow, accompanied by 4,700 troops and 32 guns. His progress was leisurely, as he did not think that the prevailing situation at the Lucknow Residency warranted any rash or hurried action on his path.

The British reconnoitring party reached Banthra (then a small non-descript village and now a bustling, upcoming suburb of Lucknow on the Lucknow-Kanpur road), where they had planned to camp and wait for Campbell. The first day was peaceful, but the next day, the party was surrounded by armed revolutionaries. The British soldiers made good their escape by diving into a *nullah* (drain), and emerging on the other side as bullets whizzed past their heads. The retreating party was again accosted by armed villagers (not soldiers), under the leadership of *zamindars* (local landlords), which resulted in heavy British casualties, including thirty either killed or wounded.

On November 5th, as the British troops advanced towards *Alambagh*, laden with provisions and ammunition, the Indian soldiers opened a volley of fire from both flanks. But this was not sustained and the British advance party was not only able to deposit the stores, they also managed to move the wounded and sick from Havelock's contingent, sending them back to Cawnpore. Communication between *Alambagh* and the Residency not being available, and it was left to Kavanagh, a British civilian, to disguise himself as a native and convey Outram's message and instruction to Campbell. Briefly, it warned Campbell not to approach the city by the disastrous approach earlier adopted by Havelock, but to consider an alternative route, by way of *Jalalabad* Fort and *Dilkusha*. Campbell heeded to the advice and leaving three hundred men to garrison *Alambagh*, proceeded towards Dilkusha on November 14.

Ahmadullah 'Danka' Shah, the victor of the Battle of Chinhat described earlier tried to dislodge the British from *Alambagh*, which continued to be a garrison under Outram's command. It consisted of about 4000 men, preparing for the second assault on Lucknow; cavalry of the Indian rebel army would gallop about in the vicinity, keeping an eye on British movements. The latter would let loose a shot or two from their nine-pounders to try and scare away the Indians (Thackeray, 1896). "Danka" Shah attacked *Alambagh* on December 22 and January 12, but he met with failure on both occasions. On January 16, 1858, a serious attack was made on Outram's position by an unknown posse of men, led by an unidentified leader dressed up like Lord Hanuman. The assault continued throughout the day, with the British using their nine-pounders in defence. Night fell, and the Indian infantry, assembled in great strength, came closer, but were scattered with British grapeshot. Although the Indian advance was successfully repulsed, the British side were left with one dead bombardier and eight wounded men. 'Danka' Shah continued with his offensive on *Alambagh* on February 15, February 21 and February 25. The last battle saw Begum Hazrat Mahal, riding an elephant and joining the forces of 'Danka' Shah. The battle went on for the entire night, and yet the British did not relinquish their hold on the *Alambagh* garrison.

The Indian side continued to pile pressure on *Alambagh* till as late as March 15, till the arrival of Jang Bahadur's mercenary soldiers from Nepal, about 9000 in number. "Danka" Shah was able to inflict heavy losses on the Nepali army on March 17, 1858. But the odds were too great against the Indian side.

The Battle at *Charbagh*

Today, *Charbagh* in Lucknow is known for its rather ornate, colonial-era railway station. Prior to 1857, it was actually a congregation of four gardens (hence the name: *char* = four; *bagh* = garden) from the times of Asaf-ud-Daula, the fourth Nawab of Awadh. Within the premises, there were many large wells, whose water was conducted by way of conduits and fountains. The garden complex had innumerable criss-crossing pathways, interconnected with each other, together with recesses and pavilions. On September 25, 1857, Havelock gathered his troops in front of *Alambagh*, having finally decided to enter Lucknow from the *Charbagh* bridge, rather than follow the circuitous route via *Jalalabad* and *Dilkusha*, which had been heavily fortified by the Indian revolutionaries. But it's not that *Charbagh* did not have its hazards. Outram took the command of the first and leading brigade, with all the artillery; Havelock was in command of the second brigade, as a backup. Later, Outram would reminisce, "*The enemy had on that occasion flanked this road under cover of long grass, and a murderous fire was poured on the column from a double-storeyed house, full of musqueteers* (sic) *and from the loop holed walls of the large surrounding gardens, from two guns that raked the road from the right flank, and another that commanded the front.*" The British doggedly pushed forward, losing a third of their artillery force in the process, due to enemy fire.

The *Charbagh* bridge spanned (and still does) an old Nawabi canal built Ghazi-ud-din Haider, in an attempt to connect the Ganges with the Gomti river. The plan came to naught, but the narrow bridge sounded a death knell for the advancing British troops. The Indian freedom fighters had six guns, including a 24-pounder which had been so positioned that they could sweep the expanse beyond the bridge as also its approach. All the houses in the vicinity were loop-holed and teemed with revolutionaries. The *Charbagh* gardens were also fortified, from where a withering firing continued to sweep on Havelock's advance. The bridge itself was so narrow that it offered no cover, neither did it permit rapid movement across it, it's span allowing only two guns to be dragged up on it. There was no doubt that the revolutionaries were in a highly advantageous and strategic position; with time almost every British soldier sustained injuries and a great number were killed. Trying their best to prevent further slaughter, the British troops attempted to charge the bridge in a body,

Fig. 8: Havelock and the Madras Fusiliers on *Charbagh* Bridge, Lucknow, Unidentified Artist (1858).

attempting to use the bayonet to clear the way, instead of attempting to drag guns along with them. But the rebels had anticipated this move and poured grapeshot on the advancing British; Lieutenant Arnold, who had led the charge fell, shot through both legs; his followers were swept under the return fire from the Indian side.

But the British too did not take this assault lying down. While Outram and one regiment were busy in trying to clear *Charbagh* of insurgents, in his absence, Neil assumed command and one officer with 10 men of the Madras Fusiliers, who charged the bridge. Excepting Havelock's son, all were swept away by the fire from the Indian soldiers. The remaining Fusiliers leaped over the prostate bodies of their comrades and wrested the guns from the Indian side, bayoneting the gunners in the process. The captured Indian guns and ammunition were thrown into the canal.

The fall of *Charbagh* bridge facilitated the entry of the British into the city of Lucknow. It also sounded the death knell for Neil. The severest loss of officers and men was faced by the 78th Highlanders as indicated in the table below. The Indian side too lost stalwarts like Mir Najaf Ali, Raja Tajammul Hussain and Mirza Imam Ali, who continued to defend *Charbagh* till their very last moments.

John Bensley Thornhill, of the Bengal Civil Service and Asst. Commissioner of Oudh, staying in the Residency, had volunteered to go out and bring in the wounded in the *Charbagh* area, as he was familiar with the area. He collected as many injured as possible in *doolies* (covered palanquins or litters), but lost his way while returning, as a result of which, the long train of *doolies* reached the *Khas Bazar* area (later named as *Doolie Square* by the British), adjacent to the *Sher Darwaza*, near the *Chattar Manzil* palace complex. Here, they were set upon by Indian freedom fighters and put to death. Thornhill himself was wounded and his right arm had to be amputated; he died later on October 12, 1857.

According to Malleson (1891), "*As our men approached the archway, a tremendous firing opened upon them. Neil, who was leading them, passed through the archway, then suddenly pulling up his horse, he directed his aide-de-camp, Gordon, to gallop back and*

Table 1: List of casualties in Havelock's army from the date of crossing the Ganges on September 19 to September 26, 1857 (Gubbins, 1858)

Regiment	Killed and Missing				Wounded			Grand Total of Loss
	Killed		Missing	Total	Officers	Men	Total	
	Officers	Men						
Staff	2	0	0	2	8	0	8	10
Madras Fusiliers	0	13	11	24	2	35	37	61
H.M.'s 5th Fusiliers	0	7	16	23	2	29	31	54
H.M.'s 64th Foot	1	0	0	1	0	10	10	11
H.M.'s 84th Foot	2	9	9	20	4	24	28	48
78th Highlanders	2	37	6	45	6	75	81	126
H.M.'s 90th Light Infantry	0	11	26	37	3	46	49	86
Sikh Regiment of Firozepoor	0	6	1	7	0	37	37	44
Volunteer Cavalry	0	3	1	4	3	11	14	18
12th Native Irregular Cavalry	1	3	0	4	0	8	8	12
Artillery	2	15	7	24	2	22	24	48
Native ditto	0	5	0	5	0	12	12	17
Total	**10**	**109**	**77**	**196**	**30**	**309**	**339**	**535**

recall a half-battery which had taken a wrong road. He remained there sitting on his horse, his head turned in the direction from which he expected the half battery to emerge, when a sepoy, who had taken post on the arch, discharged his musket at him over the parapet on the top. The ball entered his head behind the left ear and killed him." This dishonourable officer lies buried in the Lucknow Residency cemetery, flanked by the graves of Henry Lawrence who had been killed on July 4 and Rev. Polehampton, the chaplain, who had died on July 20, 1857 as a victim of cholera.

On the Indian side, the revolutionaries had not been idle. In fact, they were buoyed by the realisation that British forces, despite having entering the city, had been rendered ineffectual, and commanders such as Outram and Havelock were themselves immobile within the premises of the Residency. While Man Singh's conduct remained ambivalent, other leaders such as Hanuwant Singh, Devi Baksh, Rana Beni Madho, Raghunath Singh, Bishan Singh and Bhagwan Baksh were personally directing the military operations in and around Lucknow, the new power center of northern India, after the fall of Delhi. It was Raja Hicha Ram and Madho Singh, who had proceeded to Banthra to confront the British (see above). Lucknow had become a hotbed of politics, palace intrigues, a place where all rebel soldiers preferred to converge and congregate, under their respective leaders, with whatever arms and ammunition they could muster. The city had also become a production centre for arms and ammunition, with the meagre resources were available. *Alambagh* (see above) itself had been teeming with forces led by Raja Ram Baksh, Rao Daroga Baksh, Raja Suhuj Ram, Raja Mallo Singh and Turram Baz Khan. Valour and fortitude was the call of the hour; this, the British grudgingly acknowledged in their records and memoirs (see above). No captured rebel, even in the face of impending death through summary shooting, hanging or being blown away from guns, ever displayed fear, panic or any kind of trepidation. For them, it was a do-or-die situation against heavy odds - a fight to the finish; to resolutely sacrifice their lives in order to regain their motherland from the clutches of European hegemony and its blood-spattered rule.

The Battle of *Sikandar Bagh*

Sikandar Bagh's origins are unclear; writers surmise that an early Nawabi garden, built by Sa'adat Ali Khan, the 6th Nawab of Lucknow (1798 - 1894), might have been upgraded as *Sikandar Bagh* by Wajid Ali Shah, the last King of Awadh (1847 - 1856), in honour of one of favourite *begums*, Sikandar Mahal, but was abandoned subsequently after her death. Situated in the heart of Lucknow city today, the garden was encircled by high walls with battlements on three sides - the north side having the Gomti river as a natural boundary. Entrance was through a lofty, three-storeyed gateway (extant today, but partially re-built), surmounted by kiosks. The ruins inside do not give any indication of the past glory of the garden. Scattered information about the premises are too scanty, for drawing any concrete conclusion as to what exactly existed within the area before it was decimated. However, a description does exist from the pen of Wajid Ali Shah himself (Sarkar, 2022), which goes as follows:

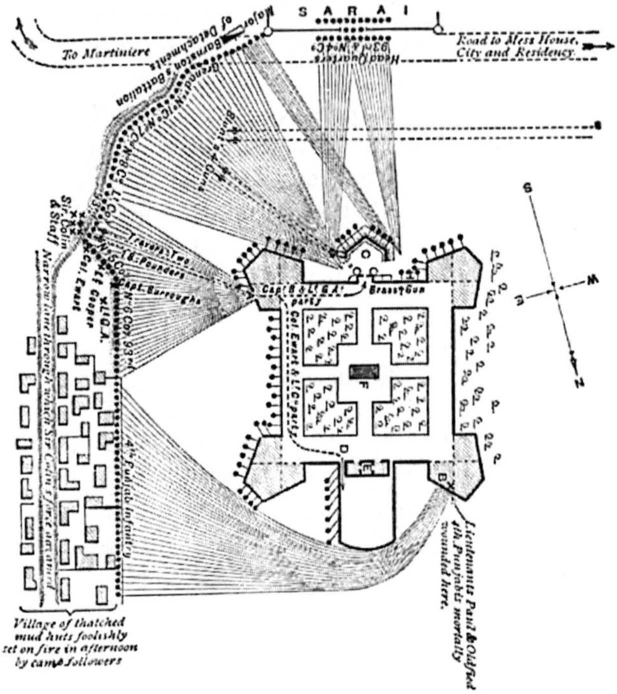

Fig. 9: Storming of *Sikandar Bagh*, Gordon-Alexander (1898).

"This garden surpassed the heavens themselves. Nawab Sikandar Mahal Saheba had occupied it during her lifetime. Since she had no heirs, the bagh became public property after her demise. Ghulam Raza Khan, Sabit Ali Khan and Kashi Ram were given charge of developing Sikandar Bagh; due to simultaneous work being carried out by several people, the building could be finished in one year's time. Otherwise, even seven to eight years would not have been sufficient. A sum of rupees five lakhs was spent on its building, but it set a precedent for others. A majestic mosque was built in the centre, which could be seen from outside. The gateway leading to the complex was so magnificent that something like this was not present in the heaven's themselves. A path led from the garden to the river. Any person standing on the balcony of the building could observe

the river from afar. The pathway was lined with fruit bearing trees on either side. And it was so wide that three carriages could pass through side-by-side, and yet some space would be available on both sides."

Fig. 10: Ruins of *Sikandar Bagh*, Unidentified Photographer (1860).

Wajid Ali's hyperbole aside, Beato's famous photograph called, "Interior of Secundrabagh (*sic*) After the Massacre" had depicted a double storeyed colonnaded building with a prominent triangular pediment, and human skeletons liberally strewn here and there. While the presence of the skeletons had created a great deal of controversy and literary discussion, the building itself was very interesting, as it was neither a palace nor a *baradari.* Also the architecture appeared to be totally European in character. In later years, the garden and its ruins were cleared by the colonial government and the "Lacknow (*sic*) Horticulture Garden" was established in a portion of the premises. The gateway was re-built and the new Outram Road, connecting Nishatganj with the city, now effectively bisected the garden into two unequal parts. Post independence, the National Botanical Research Institute was established in the premises, by the CSIR.

Sikandar Bagh saw action on November 16, 1857, in which Colin Campbell, accompanied by the 93rd Highlanders, the 4th Punjab Infantry and HM 53rd Foot stormed the premises, resulting in the slaughter of about 2200 Indian revolutionaries after a prolonged assault. Heeding to Outram's advice, Campbell had avoided the *Charbagh* bridge, and taken a circuitous route to enter the city, via *Jalalabad Fort*, *Dilkusha*, the Martiniere, *Chukkar Kothi* and finally reaching *Sikandar Bagh*. During Campbell's assault on Lucknow, the city was manned by about 53,000 revolutionaries (Mukherjee, 2001). Anticipating the second approach by British forces by the same route taken by Havelock and Neil earlier, the Indian side had mistakenly left the south-eastern flank of the fortified city completely vulnerable to British assault. This, Campbell could use to his advantage. The Indian forces stationed at *Jalalabad* and *Dilkusha* were also taken unawares. In fact, on November 13, there was a massacre at *Jalalabad*, resulting in the death of hundreds of Indian freedom fighters. The fort was also, almost completely destroyed.

It appears that the message of Outram to Campbell, as conveyed by Kavanagh (see above), had been somewhat misleading, as Outram's sources of information were not quite authentic. It had not indicated that both *Dilkusha* and *Sikandar Bagh* were strongly held by Indian rebel soldiers, and hence Campbell was somewhat complacent. An engaging, if somewhat hilarious incident, during the approach to *Sikandar Bagh* was narrated by Sgt. Forbes-Mitchell of the Sutherland Highlanders, in his reminiscences (1893):

"We saw a naked wretch, of a strong muscular build, with his head closely shaven except for the tuft on his crown, and his face all streaked in a hideous manner with white and red paint, his body smeared with ashes. He was sitting on a leopard's skin, counting a rosary of beads. A young staff-officer, I think it was Captain AO Mayne, Dy. Assistant Quarter-Master General, was making his way to the front, when a man of my company, named James Wilson, pointed to this painted wretch saying, "I would like to try my bayonet on the hide of that painted scoundrel, who looks like a murderer." Captain Mayne replied, "Oh don't touch him; these fellows are harmless Hindu jogees (ascetics) *and won't hurt us. It is the Mahommedans that are to blame for the horrors of this Mutiny." The words had*

scarcely been uttered when the painted scoundrel stopped counting the beads, slipped his hand under the leopard skin, and as quick as lightening brought out a short, brass, bell-mouthed blunderbuss and fired the contents of it into Captain Mayne's chest at a distance of only a few feet. His action was as quick as it was unexpected, and Captain Mayne was unable to avoid the shot, or the men to prevent it. Immediately our men were upon the assassin; there was no means of escape for him, and he was quickly bayoneted. Since then I have never seen a painted Hindoo, but I involuntarily raise my hand to knock him down (sic)."

The garden premises were described as a "*high walled enclosure of strong masonry, 120 yards square, and carefully loopholed all around. It was held in great strength by the enemy, and opposite to it, at a distance of hundred yards, was a village also loopholed and filled with men* (Low, 1883). A more detailed description of *Sikandar Bagh* came from Lt. Col. Gordon-Alexander (1898) of the 93 Highlanders, who had also taken part in the action there:

"The Sikandarbagh was a large enclosure, about 150 yards square, flanked at the four corners by pentagonal bastions. These bastions were occupied by two or three little rooms, each giving (sic) *by separate doors, on to the broad walk which ran along the wall all round the inside of the enclosure, and having flat roofs, with their crenulated masonry parapets heightened, strengthened and loopholed with sandbags. Owing, probably, to the greater thickness of the walls than those of the curtains* (sic)*, none of the walls were loopholed, but the intermediate walls (or curtains), joining one bastion to another, and also the walls of the back court on the north face, were all loopholed at frequent intervals and at about 4.5 to 5 feet from the ground..... the outline of the roofs of these bastions was broken by small ornamental domes and dummy minarets, but no "towers." My plan, roughly sketched on November 19, 1857, shows no building with courtyard behind it on the eastern face, but a single storied building with several rooms overlooking, none 'opening out into' a courtyard on the northern face..... not only over the whole of the main enclosure, but also in the court which jutted out from the north face, the entire surface of the open ground was thickly*

studded with the cooking-places of the high-caste Hindus (of whom the principal part of the garrison was composed)........

The only towers which ever existed in Sikandarbagh were the three towers at the gateway. One was a square tower, giving access from the garden by a narrow stone staircase to the flat roof of the gateway only, the parapets of which were loopholed and strengthened with sand-bags in the same manner as the roofs of the bastions. The other two domed towers - one on each side, and jutting outwards beyond the gateway - allowed of a flanking musketry-fire along the front curtain walls to the south-east and south-west bastions, east and west of the gate, and enclosed staircases leading to the gallery inside the gateway. The gateway itself, was flanked by these round towers, the doors and windows of which were then, of course, all built up and loopholed, was of some depth, and right and left as you entered, had first a raised platform used by the men on guard about 2.5 feet above the roadway, and above that, also on each side, at about 18 to 20 feet from the roadway, a gallery to which was access was obtained by short staircases from each of the raised platforms by the round towers. These galleries, like the platforms below, were quite open to, and overlooked, the entrance road which passed between them. The gateway itself was externally protected from artillery fire by an angular traverse of earth and brickwork, with a ditch outside some 8 to 10 feet deep and 12 feet wide at top, leaving only narrow openings, right and left, for access to the gate. In the center of the enclosure, there was a small pavilion, with a veranda running around, raised one or two steps over the broad walk which ran round it; and on the north, directly opposite the entrance gateway was a one-storied building, which overlooked the hole garden, the windows of which, as throughout the building, were not glazed, but only closed with stout Venetian shutters, to shut out the sun.

The four corners of the centre of the enclosure or garden, between the walks, were occupied by bushes and trees, some of them in huge tubs, and in peaceful times no doubt the spaces between had been filled in with flowers in pots. At the back of the one-storied building on the north face there was an oblong enclosure with walls of the same height - some 20 feet - as those which I have called the 'curtains,' joining the four bastions to each other, and enclosing the whole place. From this enclosure on the north face there was no exit to the exterior of the Sikandarbagh - meaning 'Alexander's Garden' by the way - and the only entrances to it from the main enclosure were by narrow doors situated east and west of the one storied building, which commanded this backyard from its back-windows. No door, however, opened into this yard from the building itself, which could only be entered from the main enclosure or garden."

Gordon-Alexander was appreciative of Nawabi architecture: *"The resistance of (this) brick wall to the 18-pounder shot I attribute to the tough nature of the plaster with which the bricks were coated, the finest buildings throughout India, when not of stone, having their whole surface plastered over with it, like stucco with us* (sic). *This composition, however, unlike stucco, hardens to the consistency of stone. The walls of the Sikandarbagh were nowhere more than 2.5 feet thick, yet Blunt's 9-pounders could make no impression on them, and Travers' two 18-pounders took more than an hour to hammer the small hole through which some of us entered.... like all similar 'windows' in the outer wall of the building, it had been a dummy one, moulded by the native builder for architectural effect; hence none of these apparent 'windows' could have been broken through with crowbars or such tools, any more than any other portion of the exceedingly tough outer walls."*

On reaching *Sikandar Bagh*, the British were greeted by a volley of "murderous" fire from the loop holed walls, the windows and from the flat roof of the two storeyed building in the middle of the garden (see above). From the sparse accounts available, it seems that two Indian *Risalas* or irregular cavalry, comprising of more than 2500 dare devil soldiers, together with their commanders, Fida Hussain and Sital Singh were already present within the premises. The Indians soldiers were prepared to lay down their lives for their motherland. To protect themselves from the Indian fusillade, the British soldiers were commanded to "lie low" and aim at the loop holes and batter the walls, which went on for about three quarters of an hour. The breach which was formed in the boundary wall of the garden was not sufficiently wide for a frontal assault; hence it was decided to let the Sikh regiment storm inside, led by two of their European officers. Both the officers were promptly shot dead, bringing the assault party to an abrupt halt. Out of sheer rage and desperation, and without waiting for the breach to be widened, soldiers of all seven companies with Campbell rushed forward and leaped over the wall with a yell. The Indian rebels defending *Sikandar Bagh* had no heavy guns and their muskets were no match for Campbell's heavy artillery; the enclosing walls proved to be a trap which prevented retreat. In contrast, the resources available with Campbell are obvious from his despatch (Edwardes, 1963):

"*On the head of the column advancing up the land to the left of the Secundrabagh* (sic), *fire was opened on us. The infantry of the advanced guard was quickly thrown in skirmishing order to line a bank to the right. The guns were pushed rapidly onwards, viz. Captain Blunt's troops, Bengal horse artillery, and Captain Travers' royal artillery heavy field battery.*" Campbell then continued: "*After a time a large body of the enemy who were holding ground to the left of our advance were driven by parties of the 53rd and 93rd, two of Captain Blunt's guns aiding the movement. The Highlanders pursued their advantage, and seized the barracks, and immediately converted it into a military post, the 53rd stretching in a long line of skirmishes in the open plan, and driving the enemy before them. The attack on the Secondrabagh* (sic) *had now been proceeding for about an hour and a half, when it was determined to take the place by storm through a small opening which had been made. This was done in a most brilliant manner by the remainder of the Highlanders, and the 53rd, and the 4th Punjab infantry, supported by a battalion of detachments under Major Barnston.*"

Sniper fire from the top of a large *peepul* (*Ficus religiosa*) tree in the center of the inner court of *Sikandar Bagh* resulted in the death of several British soldiers as they attempted to access the jars filled with water, kept innocuously below the shade of the tree. A shot aimed at the top of the tree brought the sniper crashing down - it proved to be a woman, armed with a pair of heavy cavalry pistols, which she had used very effectively to kill at least half-a-dozen British soldiers. It is surmised that she was one of the members of Abyssinian females who had been employed by Wajid Ali Shah for guard duty in his harem, but who had been later rendered destitute after Wajid Ali had been deposed. The carnage and blood bath during the battle of *Sikandar Bagh* has been described by many historians. A dispassionate narration by Roberts (1910) is as follows:

"The rebels, never dreaming that we should stop to attack such a formidable position had collected in the Sikandarbagh to the number of upwards of 2,000, with the intention of falling upon our right flank so soon as we should become entangled amongst the streets and houses of the Hazratganj. They were now completely caught in a trap, the only outlets being the gateway and the breach, through which our troops continued to pour. There could therefore be no thought of escape, and they fought with the desperation of men without hope of mercy and determined to sell their lives as dearly as they could. Inch by inch they were forced back to the pavilion, and into the space between it and the north wall, where they were all shot and bayoneted. There they lay in a heap as high as my head, a heaving surging mass of dead and dying inextricably entangled. It was a sickening sight, one of those which even in the excitement of battle and the flush of victory make one feel strongly what a horrible side there is to war. The wretched wounded men could not get clear of their dead comrades, however great their struggles, and those near the top of this ghastly pile of writhing humanity vented their rage and disappointment on every British officer who approached by showering upon him abuse of the grossest description.

The firing and fighting did not cease altogether for some time after the main body of the rebels were destroyed. A few got up into the guard-room above the gateway, and tried to barricade themselves in; others sought shelter in the bastions, but none escaped the vengeance of the soldiers. There were some deadly combats between mutinous sepoys and the Sikhs. Eventually all the rebels were killed, save three or four who dropped over the wall on the city side. It is to be hoped they lived to tell the tale of dauntless courage which carried everything before it."

As Lt. Frank Astley Cubitt of the 5th Fusiliers would note down in his journal:

"There were hundreds of sepoys, dead and dying, many on fire. Piled around the entrance and in every court and garden of the place, they lay in heaps, three and four deep, a suffocating, burning,

smouldering mass while many a Highlander, Sikh, 50th and a few of ours lay among them. Now and then a stray shot came from some wretch yet able to pull the trigger..."

A mere one hundred and eight British troops (including Sikh soldiers) were killed on that fateful day at *Sikandar Bagh*. The corpses of the nameless Indian martyrs were left in the open to rot, till the putrefying stench forced the British to dispose of the bodies, either by mass cremations or by simply throwing them in the nearby river. Many of the freedom fighters who were former EIC soldiers had kept their documents and parade forms in a room in the garden complex; from these, it could be ascertained that four separate regiments had occupied *Sikandar Bagh*, comprising about 2500 men. This force had been augmented by native irregulars, bringing the total number of martyrs to about 3000. Several dead Indian soldiers had leave certificates in their pockets, signed by their former British officers, clearly indicating that the former had been on leave and had later joined the insurgency, without returning to their regiments (Forbes-Mitchell, 1893).

To quote Gordon-Alexander again:

"The gateway, with its platforms, galleries, staircases and roof; the rooms and roofs of the south-west, north-west and north-east bastions; the pavilions in the center of the garden; the rooms on the ground floor and the floor above of the building on the north face; the large courtyard which projected from the north wall behind it, were choked with dead and dying to the number, it was afterwards ascertained, of a little over two thousand of the enemy. This was no imaginary estimate, because the parade and field states of the whole garrison for that morning were discovered in one of the rooms, giving a total of over two thousand men..... there were numerous armed retainers of the Oudh landowners, and even a few amazon(sic) *negresses amongst the slain.... they fought like wild cats, and it was not until they were killed that their sex was even suspected."*

The Battle of *Sikandar Bagh* had been an epic one; the Indian soldiers, overwhelmed by the sheer numbers of British troops and their superior firepower had embraced excruciating death - a shining example of valour, fortitude and love for their motherland. As Lord

Tennyson had penned just a few years prior to 1857, in a different context:

"Theirs not to make reply / Theirs not to reason why / Theirs but to do and die"

The Battle at *Begum Kothi*

The tourist or casual visitor to the posh *Janpath Market* in *Hazratganj* today is likely to be overwhelmed by the sheer range of luxury goods available, particularly *chikan* apparel, a Lucknow speciality. However, if he takes the trouble to look around, he might still discern the remnants of broken walls made of *lakhauri* bricks, co-existing behind brightly-lit shops and kiosks lined up in front. In one corner, a *masjid* can still be identified, half hidden by billboards and other commercial structures.

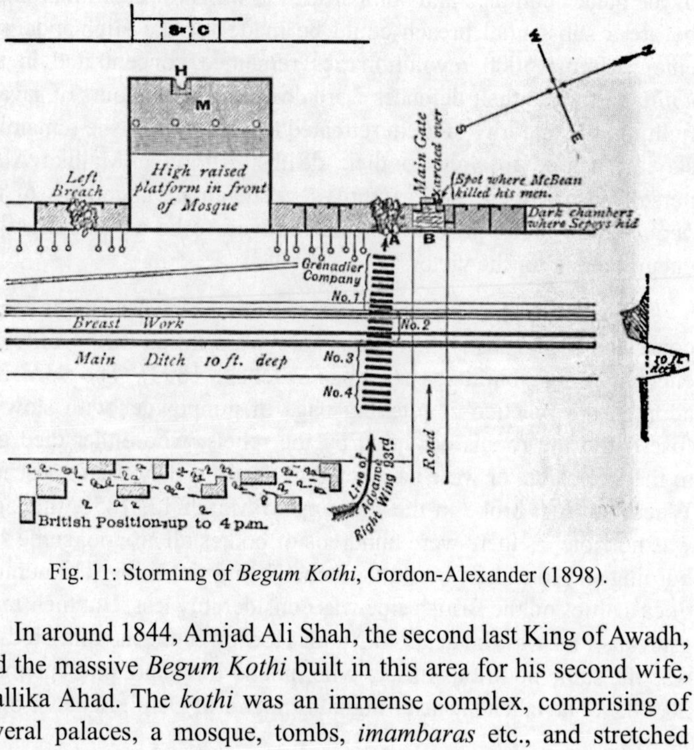

Fig. 11: Storming of *Begum Kothi*, Gordon-Alexander (1898).

In around 1844, Amjad Ali Shah, the second last King of Awadh, had the massive *Begum Kothi* built in this area for his second wife, Mallika Ahad. The *kothi* was an immense complex, comprising of several palaces, a mosque, tombs, *imambaras* etc., and stretched from the present *Vidhan Sabha Marg*, right up to the *Sibtainabad Imambara*, constituting a major portion of Hazratganj we know today. The central building was a three-storeyed structure, enclosed within high walls. During 1857 – 58, it had become a stronghold of Indian freedom fighters, thus becoming imperative for the British to seize control of the *kothi*, before they could concentrate their energies on the *Kaiserbagh*. The Indian brave hearts present in the premises included Hisam-ud-daula, Fateh-ud-Daula and Raja Jia Lal. The strongly fortified *Begum Kothi* was attacked on March 11, 1858. Along the whole front facing the British line of advance, the rebel army had constructed a ditch, about 10 feet deep and 18 feet wide. The whole palace had been prepared for defence, every gateway or passage leading from one court to another barred by traverses made with sun-dried mud, admitting only one man at a time. Peel's Naval Brigade pushed two of their heaviest guns within fifty yards of the palace complex and bombarded the walls for about four hours before a substantial breach could be made for the Highlanders to enter. Almost 5000 revolutionaries remained concentrated in the *kothi*, and when their defences were down after two hours of savage fighting, the majority of them retreated to *Kaiserbagh*, the remaining staying behind to fight to their deaths. Although Mallika Ahad herself narrowly escaped capture, several female attendants of the *begum* were taken prisoners, which proved to be an embarrassing encumbrance for the victors.

By evening, eight hundred and sixty Indians lay dead in the center court alone, and many hundreds more were killed in the different enclosures and buildings ((Forbes-Mitchell, 1893). The 93rd had adopted the practice of pitching bags of gunpowder with slow lit fuses, into the rooms occupied by the rebels, who either died due to the explosion, or were bayoneted to death, if they tried to escape. When daylight broke in the morning of March 12, 1858, the sight was horrible, as there were hundreds of bodies all around, some still burning and some half-burnt; the stench being sickening. The number of casualties on the British side was considerably less. But their most grievous loss was the death of Major Hodson in the assault. Hodson was the same notorious officer who, not so long ago, on September 20, 1857, had taken the last Mughal Emperor of Delhi, Bahadur Shah

Zafar, into custody on promise of clemency. The next day, he seized Zafar's sons, Mirza Mughal and Mirza Khizr Sultan, and grandson, Mirza Abu Bakr. On the apprehension that the angry mob following him would attack, Hodson cold-bloodedly shot down the three princes and had their heads presented to the deposed King. He purportedly defended his action thus, *"I am not cruel, but I confess I did rejoice at the opportunity of ridding the earth of these wretches. I intended to have them hanged, but when it came to a question of they or us, I had no time for deliberation."*

On March 11, 1858, Hodson's regiment (Hodson Horse) had been ordered to proceed to *Alambagh*. Mopping up operations were on at the *Begum Kothi*, when it was discovered that a room was still full of rebel Indian soldiers. Hodson barged in uninvited into the proceedings and made to enter the room, sword drawn. A shot fired from inside made short work of him. He was carried to Major Bank's House (*Kothi Hayat Baksh*, the present day Governor's House) in a *doolie* and survived the night; he breathed his last the next morning and was buried in the grounds of the La Martiniere school. His grave is extant today, being venerated by certain misguided individuals who lack the proper perspective of their own country's history.

Fig. 12: Ruins of *Begum Kothi* and its environs, Beato (1858).

Campbell apparently could not control his delight at the fall of *Begum Kothi*, and exclaimed, "I knew it! I knew it! I knew they'd do it! I knew my Highlanders would take it!"

And So It Ended: The Battle at *Musa Bagh*

Today, the ruins of a Nawabi building in the midst of rolling agricultural land, encroachments and a land-fill, on the Lucknow-Hardoi road, adjoining the upcoming Vasant Kunj colony, represents the famed *Musa Bagh* or *Moosa Bagh* of yesteryears. The ruined building inside was known as *Musa Bagh Kothi*, or *Barowen* (or *Baronne*), possibly derived from the name of the village called *Baraun* or *Baraoun*, where the building is situated. The gardens, which were laid during the times of Nawab Asaf-ud-Daula were surrounded by a high walled enclosure, partially elevated, with a steep incline towards the river on one side. *Musa Bagh Kothi* was almost wholly European in character, designed by Sa'adat Ali Khan himself, as a country house, to entertain important visitors. The premises also served as a parade ground during the reign of Wajid Ali Shah. After the annexation of Awadh, *Musa Bagh* had become a military station of the EIC, being occupied by the 4th and 7th Regiments of the Oudh Irregular Infantry, which refused to bite the new greased cartridges of the newly introduced Enfield rifles. The fateful date was May 2, 1857. The soldiers were disarmed, under the orders of Lawrence, but in no time, the revolt spread to *Madiaon* cantonment in the outskirts of the city.

After the British had regained control of Lucknow in March 1858, their first and foremost target was the capture of Begum Hazrat Mahal, whom they considered their prime opponent and enemy number one. On March 15, heeding to the advice of her followers, she decided to abandon *Kaiserbagh* palace, from where she proceeded to the *Daulat Khana Asafi*. For the personal safety of the *begum* and Birjis Qadr, her movements were shrouded in secrecy. She managed to reach the house of Sharaf-ud-Daula by a circuitous route but fearing treachery, she did not stay there for long, reaching *Musa Bagh*, where she set up her new headquarters. March 19 saw Outram launching an offensive on *Musa Bagh*. Hope Grant was directed to cannonade the palace from the left bank of the river, and at the same time, Brigadier Campbell (not Colin Campbell, who was the Commander-in-Chief) was ordered to take up position on the left front of *Musa Bagh*, ostensibly to cut off the retreat of the rebel army after they had been expelled from their positions by Outram. The towering walls of the *Bagh* still bear cannon ball holes in them. But even after a fierce battle with the rebel forces, Outram was unable to capture the *begum*, who chose to leave Lucknow and continue her battle against the British from the Awadh country side and later from Nepal. Nearly five hundred freedom fighters led by Mammu Khan, the *Daroga* (Superintendent) of Begum Hazrat Mahal's court, were killed and all their artillery were captured.

Fig. 13: *Musa Bagh*, Dodgson (1860).

Seeing the fiasco at *Musa Bagh*, Outram took upon himself to pursue the fleeing freedom fighter, as they poured out of the garden complex and killed nearly a hundred of them. Many more managed to flee, as Campbell made no effort to intercept them, due to reasons best known to himself. The Brigadier later claimed that he had "lost his way", which became the official explanation. However, another officer claimed that Campbell had moved his force in utter disregard of the advice of his guides as well as fellow officers. A British officer, Captain Frederick Wale (the eighth son of General Charles Wale of

Shelford), who was in command of the 1st Sikh Irregular Cavalry, had been fatally injured and who subsequently died on March 21, 1858. He was buried in the premises of *Musa Bagh* within an enclosure, erected by one Captain LB Jones, Acting Commandant, 1st Sikh Irregular Cavalry, as a token of regard for his officer. Other British officers killed in action were Captain Halley Hutchinson and Sgt. S. Newman. March 21 also saw the Maulvi reaching *Kashmiri Mohalla* to try and exhort the residents to continue their battle against the British, but his efforts came to naught. He then shifted camp, first to *Sa'adatganj* and finally on April 7, to *Bari,* about 30 miles away from *Musa Bagh*. From there, he left for Shahjahanpur, where death by treachery awaited him.

Chapter - V

For The Sake Of Art I - The Artists

Historical Background

In any historical research, archaeological, cartographic and epigraphic information play important roles in discerning fact from fiction. Another important element is photographic evidence. Unfortunately, the technique of photography appeared quite late, but before that, manual artwork served as important indicators of what could have happened in the past. Due to its reputation, Lucknow was fortunate enough to receive a steady stream of adventurers and travellers from Europe, many of whom were talented artists / photographers in their own right. Some even settled down in the Nawabi court, being patronised by royalty and nobility alike. Much of the artwork (but not photography) was pre-1857, so today we can glean details of Lucknow's halcyon days before the events and accompanied destruction of 1857. Few British army officers also proved their acumen by way of art and photography, which added to the wealth of information on Nawabi and colonial Lucknow. Also the art depicted unequivocally that Lucknow had an undulating and not the flat topography we see today. Aurangzeb's Mosque or *Teele Wali Masjid* occupied the highest elevation of the then developing city, but sadly, despite the impressive palaces and places of worship, the road condition of the city proper was not good (a depressing fact which had been mentioned by most travellers and visitors in their memoirs). In Chapters V and VI, we shall discuss the lives and contributions of such artists and photographers, whose efforts continue to serve as an important source of information for historians and heritage enthusiasts today on the Lucknow of yore.

Joseph Tieffenthaler was born in Bolzano, formerly part of the Austrian Empire in the year 1715. The only thing known about his early years and academic career is that he spent two years in Spain. On October 9, 1729, he joined the Society of Jesus and subsequently left for the East Indian mission in 1740. Soon after his arrival in Goa, he was appointed rector of the Jesuit High School of Agra. Besides his native tongue, he understood Latin, Italian, Spanish, French, Hindustani, Arabic, Persian, and Sanskrit. Often called the *forgotten cartographer*, he travelled extensively in north and eastern India, along the course of the Ganges (Ganga) river, focussing on correcting the previously stated geographical details of the countryside. Using a quadrant, he corrected the coordinates of cities and temples, compiling his works into two publications, *Description Indiœ* and *Cursus Gangœ*.

Tieffenthaler was one of the earliest visitors to Lucknow who attempted to describe not only the cartographic details of *Lacnau* or *Laknao* (Lucknow) and its rivers, *Goumati* (Gomti) and *Cocràl* (Kukrail) but also the *Palais Quintuple* (*Panch Mahalla*) palace complex of the *Sheikhzadas,* then a prominent structure (or principal

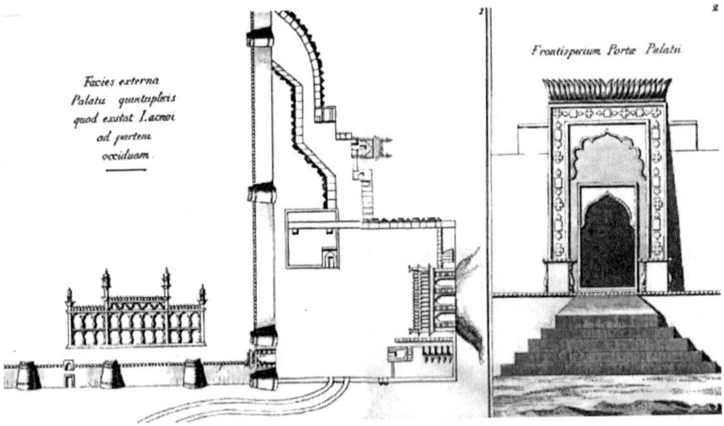

Fig. 14: Front elevation of *Panch Mahalla* palace complex, Lucknow, Tieffenthaler (1786).

Fig. 15: *Panch Mahalla* and the Gomti river, Tieffanthaler (1786).

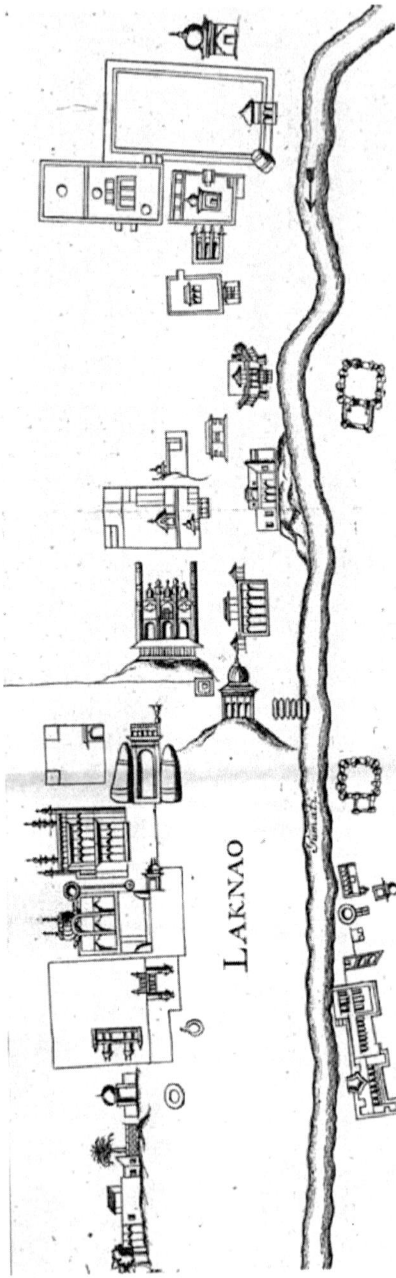

Fig. 16: Plan of Lucknow ("Laknao") with the Five Palaces and the Aurangzeb mosque at the center, woodcut print, Tieffanthaler (1765).

edifice) of the city, which would later metamorphose into the *Macchi Bhavan* citadel under Nawabi rule. In 1766, after returning from Calcutta, for the next five years (1766–1771) he remained in Lucknow. Tieffenthaler never returned to Europe and died in Lucknow, in 1785. He lies buried at the mission (*Padri Tola*) cemetery in Agra.

Captain Robert Smith: Captain Robert Smith was a military engineer with the East India Company (Royal Bengal Engineers), having arrived in Calcutta in 1805. His flair for surveying was noticed by the Surveyor General, as "*the best draughtsman I am acquainted with. His masterly rapid pencil particularly qualifies him for survey of the Frontier, as he will be able to delineate the passes and surrounding country with the greatest correctness*." Between 1812 and 1813 Smith joined the camp of the Commander-in-Chief, Sir George Nugent, for his tour of Upper India. Smith's sketches were appreciated by Lady Nugent, who noted in her diary that "Just as day dawned, we crossed the Jumna. … I took the engineer officer, Mr. Smith, with me, and we projected a drawing of the line of march, which will be a treasure to me, if he executes it according to my plan, and I have little doubt of its being quite perfect, by what I have seen

Fig. 17: The *Rumi Darwaza* and adjacent *Sunheri Burj* palace (not extant) at Lucknow, Capt. Robert Smith (1814).

of his drawings." He was next appointed as Inspecting Engineer to accompany Lord Moira (both Governor-General and Commander-in-Chief) on his tour to the Upper Provinces from May 1814, being 'selected from his character for talents and abilities'. He was with Moira until the end of 1814 when he joined General Martindell's Division in the Anglo-Nepal War of 1814-15, where he was appointed Assistant Field Engineer. Smith's panoramas of Lucknow provide fantastic details of the city, including minutae of structures which are no longer extant. These include the *Sunheri Burj* palace, adjacent to the *Rumi Darwaza* and the front elevation of the *Musa Bagh Kothi*. His sketch of *Khurshid Manzil* (1814) provided details of what the building looked like originally (present day La Martiniere College for Girls). He also produced intricate sketches of the marching equipage of the rulers of Awadh, as also their fish shape boats gliding down the Gomti. The cupola atop *Qutub Minar* at Delhi was also designed by Smith (this was later brought down, and came to be known as Smith's Folly). He remained in India from 1805 - 1833, formally retiring in November 1832, at a relatively young age of 45. Returning

Fig. 18: View of *Teele Wali Masjid* (Aurangzeb's Mosque) at Lucknow, Ozias (1786).

to Europe, he settled in Paignton, Devon, where he built his home, *Redcliff Towers*, an architectural oddity. Smith died in 1873.

Humphry Ozias was born on September 8, 1742 in Honiton, Devon County, and derived his name from his great grandfather, Rev. Ozias Upcott, Rector of Honiton. He studied art in London and Bath and moved to Italy for some time, where there was demand for his works. He became well known for portrait miniatures, oils, pastels and crayons. Ozias was active in India during 1785 - 1787. He produced many miniatures and sketches in Calcutta and then proceeded to Lucknow, hoping to paint and earn a fortune in Asaf-ud-Daula's court, where he made water colour miniatures of Haider Beg Khan and an infant Wazir Ali. However, it seems he only got a token payment and a bond for the remainder, which it so appeared that Asaf-ud-Daula had no intention of honouring. Humphry made

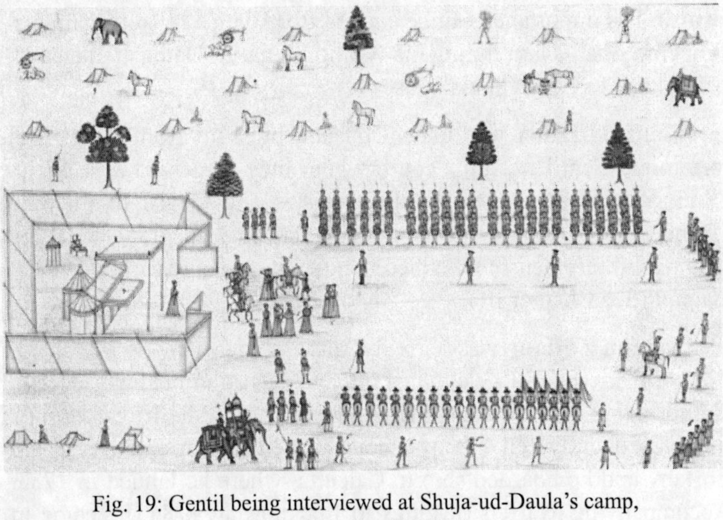

Fig. 19: Gentil being interviewed at Shuja-ud-Daula's camp, Faizabad, Gentil (1774).

another miniature during his 5 month stay at the house of John Wombwell, the East India Company's Accountant at Lucknow, dated March 13, 1786. It depicted boats and elephants by the Gomti river with the *Teele-Wali Masjid* on the opposite bank and the high walls of the *Macchi Bhavan* beyond it, parallel to the river. He left Calcutta in 1787 with an impaired health and without any fortune. Ozias had a failing eyesight, due to a fall during horse riding in 1772 and went completely blind in 1797. He died in 1810 in Hampstead, north London.

Jean-Baptiste Gentil, the French Resident of Nawab Shuja-ud-Daula in Faizabad, has been discussed in detail elsewhere in this book. Born in Bagnols, Languedoc on June 25, 1726, he served in India under various French generals *viz.* Joseph Dupleix, Charles Bussy, Jean Law de Lauriston and Comte de Lally. Later, he joined the court of Shuja-ud-Daula at Faizabad, with 200 French soldiers, literally becoming his *aide-de-camp*, advising the Nawab on diverse matters, and gradually establishing a battalion of 600 French mercenaries. Gentil made detailed maps of Mughal India, wrote treatises on historical matters, collected rare and valuable manuscripts and acted on behalf of the Nawab, particularly when negotiating with the British. His importance can be gauged from the fact that the Mughal Emperor, Shah Alam during his visit to Shuja-ud-Daula at Faizabad, paid a visit to Gentil at his house.

Shuja-ud-Daula was under constant pressure from the British to remove Gentil from his court, whom they perceived as a threat. Ultimately, Shuja bowed to their wishes and Gentil returned to Chandernagore, and by October 1777 was back in France. Having lost his military pension, he died in poverty on February 15. 1799 at Bagnol (See Chapter III).

Johann Zoffany was born in Frankfurt, Germany on March 13, 1733. He arrived in England in 1760 and was an immediate success. He got many commissions, including work from the Royal Family, but subsequently fell out of favour. The riches of India attracted Zoffany and he boarded ship to Calcutta, where he landed in 1783. Accompanying Warren Hastings to Lucknow in 1784, he came in contact with other Europeans of the Nawabi court, including Martin, Polier and Wombwell. His incredibly detailed painting, *Colonel Mordaunt's Cock Match* was the highlight of his stay in Lucknow, although he made paintings of Mughal Prince Jawan Bakht, Hasan Raza Khan and of Asaf-ud-Daula himself. Zoffany's paintings were extremely detailed and he considered his work to be historical pieces and not just observational scenes. His imagery was always dense, whether they were portraits or landscapes, e.g. the painting entitled *The Embassy of Haider Beg to Lord Cornwallis,* as also the meeting of Asaf-ud-Daula with Warren Hastings at Lucknow (Fig 20).

Fig. 20: Meeting of Asaf-ud-Daula and Warren Hastings, Zoffany (1784).

Zoffany returned to England in 1789 and continued to produce original art as well as copies of his earlier works. He died on November 11, 1810 and was buried in the churchyard of St Anne's Church, Kew.

Robert Home was born in 1752 in Kingston upon Hull (Eastern Yorkshire), England, the son of a prominent army surgeon. From an early age, he displayed no talent for medicine, but began to study art and painting instead. He sailed for India in 1791 and after establishing himself in Calcutta, proceeded to Lucknow, ultimately becoming a celebrated court artist for Ghazi-ud-Din Haider, the first King of Awadh in 1814. In addition to his access to the King himself, he was one of the privileged few who were also privy to the royal household. Along with studio portraits of royalty and nobility, both Indian and British, Home was also responsible for conceptualising and designing a diverse range of articles and objects, from the King's crown, to his dress, regalia, chairs and even the crocodile-shaped barge he travelled in. It has also been suggested that Home was involved in designing the *Chattar Manzil* palace itself, which, if true, lends credence to Home's multifarious talents and his influence in the court of Ghazi-ud-Din Haider. After the King's death in 1827, Home led a retired life in Kanpur with his widowed daughter, Anne Walker. Having spent most of his lifetime in India, Home died at the age of 82, and was interred in the *Kutchery* Cemetery of Kanpur.

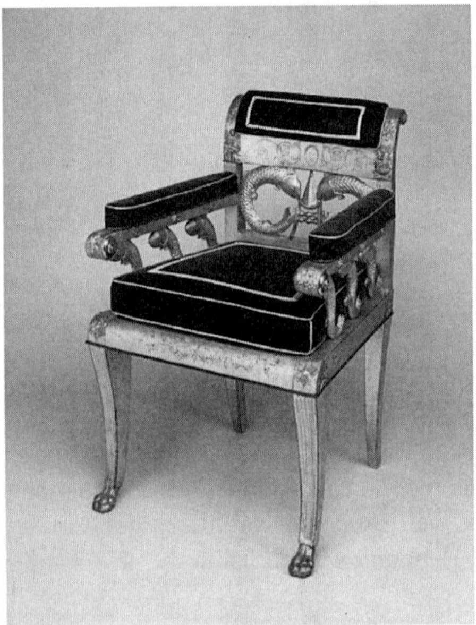

Fig. 21: Chair designed by Robert Home for Ghazi-ud-Din Haider (1820).

Henry Salt was the official artist and secretary of Viscount Valentia (George Annesley), who left England on the *Minerva*, for a grand tour of the East, in June 1802. Henry had recently finished his training with the topographical draughtsman and diarist, Joseph Farington. Valentia and Salt returned to England in 1806 and set about producing the *Twenty Four Views Taken in St. Helena, the Cape, India, Ceylon, Abyssinia and Egypt*.

Salt depicted Lucknow's famous *Asafi Masjid*, built on a two-storeyed plinth with two minarets, modelled after Delhi's *Jama Masjid*. The Viscount wrote that it was "built of brick but completely covered with so brilliant a *chunam*, that it is impossible to bear the lustre when the sun shine full upon it. The tops of the minarets and of the domes are gilt. It forms one side of a square. The other sides are composed of a palace, celebrated for a deep and wide well, the *Imaunbarah* (sic) ... and three light, fantastic gateways, with arches similar to those in the Mosque. In the centre is an Asiatic garden, divided into regular beds, by large walks of stone." Salt eventually became British Consul-General in Egypt, where he died at the age of 47.

Fig. 22: *Asafi Masjid* by Henry Salt (1809).

Sita Ram was an Indian artist trained in the contemporary Murshidabad school, but no doubt working in Calcutta during 1810-15. He accompanied Francis Rawdon, popularly known as Marquess of Hastings or Lord Moira (not to be confused with Warren Hastings), the Governor General of Bengal (1813 - 1823), who undertook a journey across eastern and north India by boat, during 1814 - 1815. The artist's work could be compiled in 10 albums, each containing 23 drawings (water colours), depicting various landscapes and monuments observed during the course of the journey. From his artistic style, it was obvious that Sita Ram had been influenced considerably by European water colourists and engravers of aquatints such as William Hodges and Thomas and William Daniell (discussed elsewhere). While the Marquess had an interview with Ghazi-ud-Din Haider, Sita Ram busied himself in capturing *Macchi Bhavan,* and other buildings, including the *Rumi Darwaza*, in his usual detailed style.

Fig. 23: *Rumi Darwaza* by Sita Ram (1814).

After the above prolonged journey, Sita Ram continued to work for Hastings. Two albums of drawings again by Sita Ram, having views of Bengal, were prepared on subsequent tours, one during a sporting expedition to northern Bengal in 1817, and another during a convalescent tour in the Raj Mahal Hills in 1820-21. However, there was no further update on Sita Ram's career after Hastings' departure from India in 1823.

Thomas Longcroft was born in 1760. A "British Old Master" artist. he reached Indian shores in 1783 and visited Lucknow with Zoffany in the following year. Zoffany was a success in the Awadh court (of Asaf-ud-Daula), but Longcroft was less fortuitous. In present times, Longcroft is known for producing elaborate artworks (Company School) depicting Indian landscapes and life. In fact, his visit coincided with the on-going construction of the *Asafi Imambara* complex at Lucknow, and one of his paintings actually depicted

Fig. 24: Lord (Hastings) Moira approaching Lucknow, Sita Ram (1814).

the scaffoldings around the under-construction *Asafi Masjid*. His "views" of Lucknow depicting palaces and streets, provide a great deal of detail, in the absence of photography in those days. Particular

Fig. 25: View of *Daulat Khana Asafi* and
Bridge of Boats across Gomti river, Longcroft (1790).

mention must be made of his depiction of the *Daulat Khana* complex from the river side. However, he was mortified to realise that his works and talents were overshadowed by Zoffany in the Awadh court. In 1787, he purchased an indigo estate at Koil, near Aligarh, (in present day UP), where he lived till the end of his days, having formed a lasting relationship with an Indian lady, Mubarak Jahan. Related to Thomas Twining of the EIC (whose family would later become famous for the marketing of tea and other beverages), who visited him in December 1794, many of Longcroft's artworks passed on to the Twining family after his death in 1811.

Tilly Kettle: Tilly Kettle was born in Silver Street, London on January 31, 1735. He was a portrait artist, active in Britain who finally left for India in 1768. Arriving in Madras in 1769, he spent about two years working in Calcutta before receiving a letter of invitation from Shuja-ud-Daula who had been told that Mr Kettle 'is a master of his art.' Kettle painted the Nawab and his sons several times during his visit to Faizabad during 1772-73, setting the trend for European artists to visit India to earn their fortunes. He was also a master in self portraits (similar to Zoffany). Kettle returned to London in 1776, and

Fig. 26: Tilly Kettle (as himself) painting Shuja-ud-Daula and his seven sons (1771).

settled there for some time. Although he was well off, and his wife, Mary "Polly" had also brought a substantial dowry, it appears that he lost his wealth and fell into debt. He tried to avoid his creditors for some time, but eventually decided to set off for India once again. However, this journey was short-lived and he died, possibly while trying to cross the desert near Basra, present day Iraq, in 1786.

Lt. Clifford Henry Mecham was the third son of Capt. George Mecham and his wife, Harriet. Born on November 24, 1831, in Liechester, he attended Jersey Collegiate School and later joined Cheltenham College. Henry joined the army in 1848 and arrived in India in 1849, to be stationed at Vellore as part of the 52nd Madras Native Infantry. In February 1856, he was appointed as Adjutant of the 7th Oude Irregular Infantry at Lucknow. In June 1857, his regiment revolted and Mecham initially remained confined in the *Macchi Bhavan* fortification, which was later abandoned. He moved to the Residency and survived a mine explosion, in which most of his compatriots were killed. It appears that his penchant to create detailed artwork, and his heavy intake of alcohol helped him to survive the trauma of the Residency siege, "looking more like a

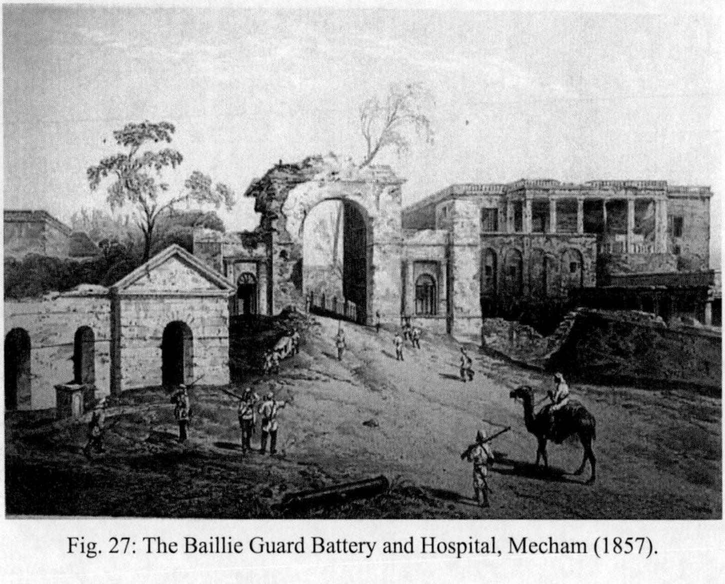

Fig. 27: The Baillie Guard Battery and Hospital, Mecham (1857).

Fig. 28: Front View of the Residency, Mecham (1857).

Fig. 29: Interior of the Residency Billiard Room, Mecham (1857).

greyhound than a man, as thin as a lathe and eyes sunken into his head" to quote Lt. Jones-Parry, his school friend. Mecham remained in Lucknow, first with the Madras Fusiliers and then Hodson's Horse. He completed the manuscript of his book, *Sketches and Incidents of the Siege of Lucknow* in 1858, the accompanying narrative being written by George Couper (who would later serve as the first Lt. Governor of the NW Provinces and Chief Commissioner of Awadh), the main purpose being to utilise the sketches made by him when the city had been besieged. In addition to the narrative of the Residency premises, both inside and outside (we come to know that there was a *Water Gate* inside the Residency premises, which presumably offered direct access to the river), Mecham also drew detailed depictions of *Alambagh* and the elusive *Jalalabad* fort, the latter having been recently described in detail by Sarkar (2021), but another interesting insight had been provided by Mecham himself, as below:

"On the extreme right of General Outram's position was the fort of Jellalabad, which was occupied by our troops, and formed a very strong post. It is almost surrounded with lakes and marshes, from which the markets of Lucknow are supplied with wild-fowl. The officers stationed here have picked up a kind of punt, in which they used to make expeditions over these extensive sheets of water in search of game; and on more than one occasion an adventurous party have narrowly escaped falling into the hands of the enemy's sowars, who rode into the shallow water, and pursued the flying sportsmen at a pace far superior to that at which their utmost exertions could propel the wretched old punt."

On September 20, 1864 he was removed from his command of the 9th Bengal Cavalry and remained unemployed until April 1865. Mecham died of hepatitis on September 15, 1865 and was buried in Ambala.

Major Macbean had been active in Lucknow during 1858. Biographical details of this soldier are not available - it is not clear whether he was the same William Macbean who was later awarded the VC for "single-handedly killing eleven of the enemy with his own sword, in the main breach of the *Begum Bagh* (sic) at Lucknow" on March 11, 1858. Like Mecham, Macbean also produced a series of sketches of Lucknow during that period and his subjects were often similar to that of Mecham. The sketches were later photographed by J. Hogarth, a London photographer, and compiled into a leather-bound book, *Views in Lucknow : From Sketches made during the Siege 1858*. His art (Fig 30), the "Palace of the former King of Lucknow" is interesting, possibly depicting *the Chota Chatter Manzil* (Fig. 46) as it is too small to be the *Bada Chattar Manzil.* Macbean also sketched the Residency proper, and its environs, including the Nawabi *Latkan Darwaza* or Clock Tower Gate.

Macbean's most evocative artwork was that of state prisoners confined within the Residency premises. They included Mustafa Ali, (the eldest son of Amjad Ali Shah) who is depicted as sitting on a bed in the back of the room to the left. Syed Khadim Hussein (an official of late Nawab Ghazi-ud-din Haider), is sitting on a striped rug on the floor, wrapped in a white cloth. Mirza Muhammad Humayun Shah (a Mughal prince) is standing at the centre of the group with his hands together. Mirza Muhammad Haider Shikoh (another Mughal prince), is sitting at the back of the room. The Rajah of Tulsipur, is lying on a bed to the far right covered with a blanket. It is surmised that these people had been taken prisoner, as a security measure, even before the siege had commenced.

Fig. 30: "Palace of former King of Lucknow", Major Macbean (1858).

Fig. 31: State Prisoners held during the Siege of Lucknow, Maj. Macbean (1858).

The Daniells, Thomas and William, were English landscape painters, who also painted Orientalist themes. They spent seven years in India, publishing several series of aquatints of the country's landscape, heritage buildings and people. The Daniells reached Lucknow as guests of Claude Martin and were introduced to Asaf-ud-Daula by the Frenchman. The artists enjoyed the hospitality of the Nawab and were encouraged to produce a series of artworks (aquatint engravings) on Lucknow, similar to their earlier work on *Views of Calcutta*. The artists remained in Lucknow for three months and produced masterpieces such as *The Punj Mahalla Gate*, *Palace of The Nawab*, *View of Lucknow taken from the opposite bank of the River Gumti, Elephants Fighting - The King of Oude and Company Looking From The Bungalow Upon The Struggle*, *Mausoleum at Lucknow* and *Garden of The Palace.* They also visited Faizabad and produced artworks depicting *Shuja-ud-Daula's Garden, Gate of the Loll-Baug* (Lalbagh) among others.

Fig. 32: "The *Punj Mahalla* Gate, Lucknow", William Daniell (1790).

William Hodges was born on October 28, 1744 in London. He was employed as an errand boy in Shipley's drawing school, where he learnt to draw in his spare time. During his early career,

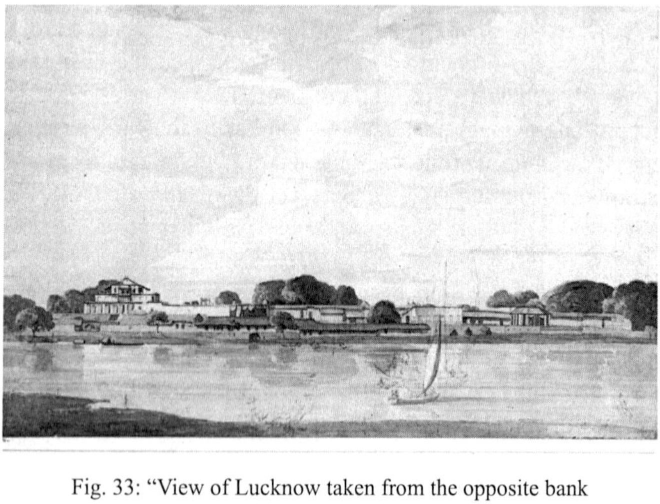

Fig. 33: "View of Lucknow taken from the opposite bank of the River Gumti", Thomas Daniell (1789).

he made a living by painting theatrical scenery. Between 1772 and 1775, Hodges accompanied James Cook to the Pacific islands as the latter's expedition artist. He worked as a landscape painter, securing the patronage of the Governor General, Warren Hastings. Journeying throughout India between 1780 and 1783, he succeeded in creating the first "views" of British India, portraying the tropics as unique and exotic. He was the first accomplished landscape artist to show topographical views of the terrain. His oil paintings and prints were acclaimed and bought by audiences at home and by British officials in India for his unorthodox use of light, shade, and atmosphere, incorporating aesthetic elements into sceneries. Thus, we may conclude that the evolution of this genre was influenced by Hodges' travels to India and his depiction of the environment in a manner that differed greatly from how contemporary British landscape artists were treating the subject at that time. Hodges was a personal guest of Claude Martin and Antoine Polier at Lucknow in 1783, although his efforts were directed more towards the ruins of the palaces in Faizabad, rather than Lucknow. The subject of the present artwork (Fig. 34) of Lucknow as described by Hodges was as follows:

The palace of the Nabob is on a high bank, near to the river, and commanding an extensive view both of the Goonty (sic) *and the*

Fig. 34 : "A View of the Palace of the Nabob Asoph ul-Dowlah at Lucknow", Hodges (1783).

country on the eastern side.... The exterior of the building is not to be commended; it reminded me of that I had imagined might be the style of a Baron's castle in Europe, about the twelfth century, close to the palace, divided by a narrow dirty or dusty road, is a garden, lately made by the Nabob, walled round, and at each angle is a grand pavilion, built of brick, and covered with chunam or stucco, and then painted with ornaments, which at a little distance has a rich effect. I have introduced a View of the Palace: on the foreground of the picture is one of the pavilions, and on a high bank is a mosque, with two minarets; and adjoining is a durgaw, or burial place, with a view of the river."

Hodges retired to Devon, but due to financial troubles, reportedly committed suicide with an overdose of laudanum.

William Simpson was a Scottish war artist and war correspondent. Born into poverty in Glasgow, Simpson became a leading 'special artist' of his time, sketching many scenes of war from across the world for the Illustrated London News. In the late 1850s, he was deputed to India by M/s Day & Sons, London, to produce artwork

Fig. 35: "Storming of the *Shah Nujeef*", Simpson (1861).

Fig. 36: "The *Dilkoosha*, Lucknow in The Distance" Simpson (1861).

relating to the recent events of 1857. Simpson arrived at Calcutta on October 29, 1859, and travelled through Punjab, Bengal, Lucknow and Cawnpore (Kanpur) among other places. Before leaving, he had visited the library of India House at Leadenhall Street, perusing books on India, such as the Daniells', to know what had been done previously and where. Although Simpson had arrived in India after the events of 1857 were over, it goes to his credit that he produced picturesque, full colour artwork on the battle scenes at Lucknow (e.g. *Shahnajaf*), based on his imagination and research. Some of his artwork had aerial views, e.g. the Residency and *Dilkusha* which was a novel approach in those days. In February 1862, he left Bombay and arrived in London; a large volume of his colour lithographs was subsequently published under the title *India Ancient and Modern*. Simpson married Maria Eliza Burt late in life, who was herself a portrait artist. He died at home in Willesden, North London, on 17 August 1899, and was buried in Highgate Cemetery.

David Scott Dodgson, son of Rev. J. Dodgson was born in 1822. He joined the army in 1838 (Bengal Infantry), ultimately becoming a General in 1888. He was active in the Jodhpur campaign of 1839 and in the Afghan War under General Pollock, 1842. Dodgson was Brigadier Major at Benares when the native troops mutinied on June 4, 1857. He remained with Havelock's force during the First Relief of Lucknow and subsequent defence, in the occupation of *Alambagh* and during the re-capture of the city in 1858. Dodgson was knighted in 1896 and died in 1898. Today, this British officer is better known for his sketches of Lucknow than for his military successes. His vividly illustrated book, *General Views & Special Points of Interest of the City of Lucknow, From Drawings Made on the Spot*, consisting of 27 tinted lithographed views Lucknow on 11 plates and one lithographed map, was published in 1860. Dodgson covered a wide range of locales, including the Residency, Iron Bridge (not extant now), Major Bank's House, *Moti Mahal*, the *Shahnajaf,* Constantia, *Dilkusha*, *Musa Bagh* and *Khurshid Manzil.* These illustrations yield important information, *e.g.* we come to know that Major Bank's House (present day Governor's House or *Raj Bhavan*) had a gate, which is no longer extant. Or that the *Moti Mahal* was not surmounted by a single pearlescent dome in the middle, but had four domes in four corners, and it was approachable by an imposing, turreted gateway. His *River View of Buildings* exhibits a detailed panorama, depicting the *Kadam Rasul*, *Shahnajaf*, *Chattar Manzil* palaces and the mausolea of Sa'adat Ali Khan and Khurshid Zadi.

Thomas Barker Jones, born in 1815 obtained his initial training in art from his father, Thomas Barker before enrolling in Horace Vernet's Parisian Studio in 1834. Barker consistently contributed to the Royal Academy and the British Institution after his return to England from France in 1845, displaying historical, literary, and hunting subjects. Unfortunately, he was not appreciated by contemporary art critics and the Royal Academy did not honour him with a Membership. However, he achieved significant commercial success for his later work, particularly as a military artist. His singular painting, *The Relief of Lucknow 1857* or *The Meeting of The Generals* (1859), as it is popularly known, was rich in architectural detail. It depicted Havelock, Outram, Inglis and others greeting Colin Campbell, against the backdrop of the *Moti Mahal* palace complex. Interestingly, the painting shows the signature turret(s) of the Moti Mahal gateway surmounted with golden cupolas, and are not bare, as in Beato's photograph, or Dodson's sketch. The artwork also shows

Fig. 37: Major Bank's House, Dodgson (1860).

Fig. 38: "Motee Mahal", Dodgson (1860).

Fig. 39: "River View of Buildings", Dodgson (1860).

Fig. 40: The Relief of Lucknow 1857 or The Meeting of The Generals, Jones (1859).

another pair of stout columns *in front of the turreted gateway*, which have never been photographed or sketched by any other photographer / artist. The full colour painting also shows the *Chattar Manzil* palace complex and the tombs of Sa'adat Ali Khan and Khurshid Zadi is stark relief. Barker died in 1882 and was buried in Highgate Cemetery.

Other one-off artworks of those turbulent times at Lucknow by Louis-Henri de Rudder, Lt. General Ezekiel Barton, Edward Lear, Prince Aleksei Soltykov, Earl George James Howard, Charles D'Oyly, Thomas Murray, William Carpenter, CE Watson, Charles Ulrich. Orlando Norie, Henry Payne, Robert Orr, Louis William Desanges, John Frederick Cheetham, James Ross, PC Geissler, Howard Davie, Cecil Philip Lawson, Frederick Shoberl, George James Howard, Charlotte Schreiber, Helen Messinger Murdoch, Alexandre Benoit Jean Dufay Casanova, Lt. Col. Charles Ramus Forrest, Emily Eden, Henry Hope Crealock, Marjorie Sherlock, Cordelia Ellen Thomas and Nicholas Chevalier, may not have been so informative or evocative, but nevertheless they remain collectors' items, since they depicted the dazzle as well as travails of a city and its people who, from leading a content, if dissolute life-style, were sucked into the maelstrom of an armed revolution, which benefited nobody in the long run.

Chapter - VI

For The Sake Of Art II - The Photographers

Pre-1857 Scenario

Baron Alexis de La Grange was perhaps the first European having photographic skills, to travel to India in the early nineteenth century. Born in an aristocratic French family in 1825 (the son of an army colonel, Baron Prosper Amauri Louis, who was an officer of the Ordre national de La Légion d'honneur), de La Grange studied in Paris at the Ecole Polytechnique (1844), before embarking on a two years trip to India and south-east Asia. He met Maxime Du Camp in Egypt in 1849; the latter taught him the use of Blanquart-Evrard's wet paper negative process in photography.

Photographic techniques were in their developmental stage in those early days of photography, and the final output did not have the effective imagery and detail (including colour) that paintings could provide (discussed in the previous Chapter). Grange's panoramic view (Fig. 41), focusing on the *Rumi Darwaza* and its environs was hazy and unclear; nevertheless, in the absence of any further evidence, it can be accepted to be the first photograph of Lucknow, although photography had appeared on Indian shores by 1840. La Grange's pre-1857 photograph of the *Asafi Masjid* clearly depicted the mosque's original appearance, complete with small chambers (*ghulam gardish*) on the ground floor or plinth level, like the early artwork of Henry Salt and Sita Ram; these would later be covered under an artificial mound and a wide stairway built over it after 1857 under British supervision.

Fig. 41: Panorama of Lucknow, Alexis de La Grange (1849).

Ahmad Ali Khan is considered to be the first *native* photographer of Lucknow. He possibly picked up skills in still photography from de La Grange himself, soon becoming a much sought after photographer, acquiring access to the Nawabi court, including the *zenana* or female quarters. Thus, from being an architect (of considerable talent) in the court of Mohammad Ali Shah (*Hussainabad* complex) and Wajid Ali Shah (*Kaiserbagh* complex), he re-invented himself as a royal court photographer, during the last days of Nawabi rule, holding the official title of *Daroga* (Superintendent). Ahmad Ali's was also a favourite in British circles, the most significant aspect of his work being that he did not accept any payment for services provided. As could be expected, his sympathies lay with the revolutionaries during the uprising, which resulted in his becoming *persona non grata* in the eyes of the British. Consequently, his house was raided by British soldiers and two boxes of glass negatives confiscated, which ultimately reached Scotland, from where they remained untraceable till date. After the uprising was over, Khan resumed his hobby, capturing both architectural views and portraits in Lucknow, using his original nondescript *nom de plume* as *Chote Mian*. Khan's view of post-1857 *Chattar Manzil* clearly depicted that the river had changed course and moved away from the palace. The piers on the north side of *Chattar Manzil* and neighbouring *Farhat Baksh* no longer jutted out into the river but were buried in the soil. A crude embankment had been made, possibly to prevent flood waters from entering the premises. The slow and steady deterioration of the palace complex had begun.

Fig. 42: *Chattar Manzil* and *Farhat Baksh*, Ahmad Ali Khan (1860).

The Uprising: 1857-58

Patrick Fitzgerald's photograph of victorious British soldiers lounging on the roof of *Alambagh Kothi* was perhaps the first "war-time" photograph of Lucknow. Fitzgerald was not a soldier but a medical doctor, accompanying Havelock's relief force.

Lt. Col Owen Mortimor Lanyon captured a similar view of the roof top of *Alambagh Kothi*. His collection also included a photograph of the *Alambagh* gate, together with a view of the area, from atop *Alambagh* gate, showing the mango trees under which Havelock had been buried in haste. This was the phase when British soldiers also acted as amateur photographers, while simultaneously fighting the revolutionaries.

Lance Corporal EW Jones of the Royal Engineers, produced a handful of albumen prints (12 nos. to be exact) from collodion negatives, most of which were of Lucknow, during and after its recapture in March 1858. Jones was one of the few photographers who was present to capture scenes at the time of the actual fighting.

Fig. 43: Soldiers atop *Alambagh Kothi,* OM Lanyon (1858).

If the reader is taken by surprise by the photographic talent of British soldiers, it needs to be clarified that the Royal Engineers (RE) and its Company equivalents had introduced photography to both officers and NCOs by the mid-1850s. From 1855, training in photography was available to cadets at the Company's Addiscombe College, and by 1858, at least one RE unit, the 23rd, were provided with a camera as routine equipment.

Fig. 44: Ruins of *Chattar Manzil* (north side), OM Lanyon (1858).

Captain J. Milliken produced several architectural views of war time Lucknow. His depiction of the north facade of *Musa Bagh Kothi* remains highly informative, since the *kothi* is in a derelict condition today.

Fig. 45: *Musa Bagh Kothi,* Capt. J. Milliken (1858).

Fig. 46: *Chota Chattar Manzil*, Col. Montague Hall (1858).
(Compare with Fig. 30)

Col. Montague Hall compiled an album of 99 items including photographs, watercolours, press cuttings and prints, spanning the period of 1853-1878. It is not clear if they were his own or some other officer's output, since no names were indicated. Nevertheless, the architectural views therein were unique and provided new insights of buildings (and their ruins e.g. *Chota Chattar Manzil*, *Alambagh Kothi* and the *Shahnajaf.*

Lt. Richard Stainforth was born in Pontefract, Yorkshire on the 30th of September, 1839. As part of his 56th Bengal Native Regiment had mutinied at Cawnpore (Kanpur) on the 5th of June, 1857, Stainforth was attached to other regiments during the early part of the uprising in India. He died in 1865 at the age of 26, leaving behind a rich collection of memorabilia connected with 1857, which included a hand-drawn map, battle orders, and small cdv (*cartes de visite*) photographs of Lucknow.

Fig. 47: *Dilkusha,* Lt. Stainforth (1858).

Fig. 48 : *Hussainabad,* Lt. Stainforth (1858).

Fig. 49: View of *Kaiserbagh*, Lt. Stainforth (1858).

Fig. 50: Vinery of *Kaiserbagh*, Lt. Stainforth (1858).

Post 1858 Scenario

Felice Beato, also known as Felix Beato, was a well-known photographer of Italian-British origin, who created several panoramas of architecture and landscapes of Asia and the Mediterranean. Born in 1832 in Venice, he was a prolific traveller and specialised in "war photography", focussing mostly on the destructive effects of war across the globe. He arrived in Calcutta in 1858 and travelled throughout northern India, photographing war torn Delhi, Kanpur, Meerut, Lahore and of course, Lucknow, where he remained for few months. His works provided authentic photographic evidence of monuments and archaeological details, immediately in the aftermath of the First War of Independence. Many of these ruins would later be torn down; hence Beato's work effectively documented photographic details of structures, which would disappear in due course of time. Beato's evocative treatment of *Sikandar Bagh* is well known in

Fig. 51: Ruins of *Macchi Bhavan*, Beato (1858).

Fig. 52: Lucknow in ruins, Beato (1858).

photographic circles across the world and need not be re-iterated here with all its gory (if dramatised) details. Similarly, his panorama of *Macchi Bhavan* and *Kaiserbagh* remains unsurpassed till today, providing a wealth of architectural information on structures that have vanished with time. Beato would later carry out similar works in China, Japan and Burma. He died in Florence in January 1909.

Donald Horne Macfarlane was born in Caithness, Scotland, in June, 1830. He arrived in India in 1859 as a partner in M/s Begg, Dunlop and Co., Calcutta. Initially, he was based at Cawnpore, then left for Calcutta in 1860. His candidature was proposed for Membership of the Bengal Photographic Society in 1860, where he exhibited prints taken in Lucknow, the N.W. Provinces and Calcutta; Donald was awarded the Society's gold medal for landscapes and silver medal for best single photograph in 1861, with the citation that, "Mr MacFarlane exhibited a stereoscopic camera with Dallmeyer's instantaneous shutter, a highly finished instrument, which was

Fig. 51: *Gulistan-e-Iram, Chota Chattar Manzil and Darshan Bilas,* Francis Frith (1860).

much admired; also some instantaneous views in Calcutta, in which moving figures and carriages were very perfectly rendered. These are

Fig. 54: *Roshan-ud-Daula Kothi / Kaiser Pasand*, Francis Frith (1860).

believed to be the first really instantaneous views taken in India ever exhibited to the Society. He was in India for a mere seven years, from 1863 to 1870. But he took thousands of pictures and established a lucrative business. His photograph of *Macchi Bhavan* at Lucknow, seen together with the Tytlers' (discussed later) photograph gives us an indication on what the citadel might have looked like, before being demolished by the British.

Francis Frith was born in Chesterfield in October 1822. In 1850, he started a photographic studio in Liverpool. Within a short time, he became extremely proficient in the art and undertook several journeys, visiting Egypt, Palestine, Syria and India. Frith's photographs were compiled into illustrated books, which were highly in demand. His firm, Francis Frith & Co., was the world's first photographic studio and publisher. For India as a whole, Frith had a collection of 1,445 photographs, out of which 23 were of Lucknow.

Mushkoor-ud-Daula and **Asghar Jaan**, the brother duo, were prominent Indian photographers, in the post 1858 phase of Lucknow, during colonial rule. Unfortunately, the brothers' photographic output continues to remain scattered and undocumented. Referred to as *Mushkooroodowlah* on several photographs of mostly (and surprisingly) nautch girls or *tawa'ifs*, their work was supplemented by a contemporary photographer, one Musaddi Lal or *Musuddeelal,* of *Sadur Bazar* (sic), Lucknow.

Fig. 55: Pavilions on the Gomti, Mushkoor-ud-Daula (1860).

Mushkoor-ud-Daula's view of the ruins of the pavilions on the river Gomti, takes one back to the happier times of Sa'adat Ali Khan, when the pavilions were ornate, two storeyed structures, surmounted with the ubiquitous *chattris,* so favoured by the Nawabi regime. The pavilion in the middle of the river would be equipped with a jetty, and the ruling Nawab would spend leisurely evenings, fishing and enjoying the cool breeze of the river.

Samuel Bourne was an acclaimed British photographer, famous for his extensive work in India, during 1863 to 1870. Together with Charles Shepherd, he established a photographic studio, M/s Bourne & Shepherd, first in Shimla in 1863 and later in Calcutta, where a majority of this work was unfortunately destroyed in the infamous fire of 1991. Bourne is often regarded as one of the finest landscape and travel photographers of nineteenth-century India, due to his

Fig. 56: Beautiful Lucknow Girl, Mushkoor-ud-Daula (1865).

Fig. 57: A Courtesan of Lucknow, Musaddi Lal (1870).

fine eye for composition combined with high technical expertise. With its closing down in June 2016, the studio had operated continuously for 176 glorious years. Bourne's numerous photographs and bird-eye views of Lucknow city, post 1857, amply indicate the landscaping operations that the British had conducted after they had regained control of the city. While demolishing a vast majority of Nawabi structures, they had retained few for their own use, which were spruced up and beautified. Fig. 58 depicts the *Chota Chattar Manzil* palace, which is no longer extant and the *Darshan Bilas*, which, even in its present restored *avatar*, is nowhere near to what it looked like in the 1860s, after being restored by the British.

John Edward Saché's origins are unclear; he reached Calcutta in 1864, following the footsteps of Bourne. Indeed, some of his works are confused with that of Bourne's, unless signed by him. He opened his own studio in Nainital in 1867, and by 1868, had compiled a substantial selection of photographic prints of Delhi, Cawnpore, Lucknow, Calcutta and others locations. Lucknow had a unique, if somewhat morbid attraction for the British, who were particularly

Fig. 58: *Chota Chattar Manzil* (left) and *Darshan Bilas* (right), Samuel Bourne (1864).

Fig. 59: The Residency, Samuel Bourne (1864).

interested in photographs of monuments damaged during the 1857 carnage, cenotaphs built after the uprising, and locations where massacres had taken place. Lucknow's decaying Nawabi architecture, was also a British favourite. The greater part of Saché's work that has survived until now was produced between 1864 and 1873. His incredibly detailed photograph of Khurshid Zadi's tomb, from atop the *maqbara* of Sa'adat Ali Khan not only shows the monument and its environs in all its glory, it also manages to present a panorama of Lucknow in the process. The photograph clearly shows the ground floor of the tomb at plinth level, which would be subsequently buried under a man-made mound by the British (as in many other structures, including the tomb of Sa'adat Ali Khan), thus effectively reducing the number of floors of the structure.

Harriet Christina Tytler and **Robert Christopher Tytler** were residents in the military cantonment in the outskirts of Delhi, when Robert's regiment, the 38th Bengal Native Infantry, was attacked by the armed revolutionaries in 1857. Harriet, a British artist, writer, and a pioneer woman photographer stayed behind with her husband, as she was expecting. Born in Sikraura, Bahraich, India, she was Robert's second wife. Harriet had been trained in still photography

Fig. 60: Tomb of Khurshid Zadi, Saché (1864).

Fig. 61: Ramparts of *Macchi Bhavan*, Robert and Harriet Tytler (1858).

Fig. 62: The *Lanka*, *Kaiserbagh*, Robert and Harriet Tytler (1858).

by Beato himself. The husband and wife team later travelled through Delhi, Cawnpore (Kanpur), Agra and Lucknow and other places affected by the uprising, ultimately producing a voluminous body of work, in about 500 waxed paper negatives. The Tytlers' photograph of the ramparts of *Macchi Bhavan* (Fig. 61), with unique boot shaped buttresses give an idea of what the boundary walls of the citadel might have looked like. The Tytlers' other high resolution photographs of the *Lanka* (Fig. 62), the Mermaid Gate, *Dilaram Kothi* and the river pavilions as well as the ruins of *Kaiserbagh* (Fig. 63), with the *Pari Khana* in the background and its marble bridge in the foreground provide invaluable photographic evidence of what these structures would have looked like before they were demolished.

Fig. 63: Marble Bridge and *Pari Khana*, *Kaiserbagh*, Robert and Harriet Tytler (1858).

Daroga Abbas Ali (1874) published a volume, containing photographs, together with short write-ups of old Lucknow buildings called *The Lucknow Album, Containing A Series of Fifty Photographic Views of Lucknow And Its Environs.* In the same year, he published another album called *The Beauties of Lucknow* in English and *Ḥasina-e-Lakhnau* in Urdu, "consisting of twenty four selected photographed portraits of the most celebrated and popular living histrionic singers, dancing girls, and actresses of the Oudh Court and of Lucknow." Later, Abbas Ali (or Ubbas Ali) published another photographic listing of the *rajas* and *ta'aluqdars* of Awadh titled *An Illustrated Historical Album of The Rajas and Taaluqdars of Oudh* (1880). This does not necessarily mean that his photographs were of the same period; it merely indicated their dates of compilation and publication. In fact, he had been active before and after the events of 1857, although, being a government municipal engineer, his sympathies apparently lay with the British.

Abbas Ali's photographs of old Lucknow buildings continue to be an importance source of information on the subject, even today. But his compilation of the beauties of Lucknow was rather controversial. It can be safely surmised that the ladies actually belonged to the *Parikhana* of Wajid Ali Shah, although they may have been dispossessed later, with the winding up of the *Parikhana* establishment and the events of 1857. That many of the *paris* had absolutely no compunction about appearing in public (which rankled Wajid Ali), it would be no great surprise for the reader that they agreed to pose before the camera of Abbas Ali at some point of time. And

Fig. 64: The Iron (Rennie's) Bridge, Lucknow, Abbas Ali (1874).

the photographer / engineer managed to get the collection published after he had retired from active service, because the work had been adulatory of the Nawabi era in an oblique manner.

Another alternative narrative could be that Abbas Ali staged an elaborate pantomime - collecting girls (not necessarily dancers), providing them with appropriate costumes and paraphernalia, photographing them and providing fake captions. But the latter theory (as proposed by some writers) seems to be highly improbable and pointless.

Fig. 65: Jaddan (Juddun), Abbas Ali (1874).

Fig. 66: Pyari (Pearee), Abbas Ali (1874).

Lala Deen Dayal was born in Sardhana, near Meerut, UP, in a family of Jain jewellers. He was a qualified engineer and worked as a draughtsman in Indore, simultaneously taking up photography as a hobby. Observing his talents, the Maharaja of Indore encouraged Deen Dayal to set up his own studio in Indore. As his business expanded, he established studios in Secunderabad and Bombay. Deen Dayal received commissions to photograph the Governor General's

Fig. 67: *Chattar Manzil* Palace, Lucknow, Lala Deen Dayal (1880).

tour of Central India; he was also assigned to photograph temples and palaces of India, assisting Sir Lepel Griffin on an architectural tour of the country. The Nizam of Hyderabad conferred the honorary title of *Raja* upon him. Deen Dayal was appointed photographer to Queen Victoria in 1897. In 1905–1906, Raja Deen Dayal accompanied the Royal Tour of the Prince (later King George V) and Princess of Wales. The mid-1880s saw Deen Dayal retiring from government service and travelling to north India, where he documented historical sites of Delhi, Agra and Lucknow, as well as photographing visiting British dignitaries with their entourages. He passed away on July 5, 1905.

Chapter - VII

The Fourth Estate

Historical Background

In contrast to exquisitely hand-written manuscripts and folios during the medieval period, print technology received a fillip with the arrival of typographic and lithographic printing, which not only took away the tedium of hand composing, it also facilitated mass publication, ensuring an extensive reach. Books (and later periodicals) were not confined to the elite now; reasonable cost and acceptable (but not overworked or overdone) quality now ensured that the common man too had access to print media. This, in turn, resulted in greater awareness, as distribution and circulation boomed. The print media had come of age as an instrument of social transformation through greater public awareness. Serialised publications, which later metamorphosed into "newspapers", that too in Urdu (not Persian / *Farsi)*, a language that had become increasingly popular in northern India, particularly in the Indo-Gangetic plains, thrived due to their ability to communicate in the language of the common populace.

Ghazi-ud-Din Haider, the first king of Awadh is credited for setting up a typographic press called *Matba-e-Sultani* (Royal Press) in 1817 at Lucknow. However, the real fillip in publishing came to Lucknow in 1830, with Nasir-ud-Din Haider (second king of Awadh) inviting Henry Archer to shift his lithographic press from Kanpur to Lucknow. By the late 1830s, lithographic presses started to proliferate under private players like Haji Harmain (Mohammadi Press) and Mustafa Khan (Mustafai Press). The 1850s saw at least twelve private lithographic presses operating with aplomb in Lucknow. However, a whimsical order of Wajid Ali Shah to shut down all printing presses, only to re-open later under close governmental censorship resulted in a severe setback to Lucknow's publishing history. It may be kept in mind that this phase of publishing in Lucknow (as elsewhere in India) was mostly confined to religious books, translations and treatises. The usage of Urdu as the common man's language, a sort of *lingua franca*, made rapid strides from 1837 onwards, with the importance of Persian (*Farsi*) diminishing rapidly and Hindi or Hindustani struggling to find its place under the sun. Hindi's print industry could finally emerge from the shadows in the late 1860s.

Apart from books, one of the earliest newspapers to emerge from Lucknow was the *Lakhnau Akhbar* in 1847. However, the advent of the printed newspaper actually occurred with the British annexation of Awadh in February 1856, but suffered a severe setback in less than a year, with the events of 1857. We shall now discuss few interesting newspapers of Lucknow, which emerged during this tumultuous period and left their mark, before fading into oblivion.

Tilism-e-Lakhnau

Fig. 68: Masthead of *Tilism.*

Firangi Mahal had been a cluster of pre-Nawabi houses in the Chowk area, dating back to the 1640s. These had been occupied by *firangs* (European) tradesmen, but it is unclear whether they were early Dutch or French or even British immigrants. In any case, they seemed to have run out of options and their property was confiscated by the Mughal Emperor, to be handed over (*madad-i-ma'ash*) to a renowned Islamic scholar, Mulla Qutub-ud-Din. The descendents of Qutub-ud-Din founded a Center of Learning within the premises of the *Firangi Mahal*. Ironically, over the next two and half centuries, the *Firangi Mahal* was to become a renowned Center for Islamic theology, its influence spreading far and wide beyond the city of Lucknow.

Tilism, as it was popularly known, was first published on July 25, 1856, at Mohammadi Press, by Maulvi Mohammad Yakub Ansari, an *ulema* (a scholar having specialised knowledge of Islamic theology) of *Firangi Mahal.* Written in Urdu, by then the language of the masses, it routinely covered local events of Lucknow city, as well as notifications of the East India Company. Borrowing news items from other newspapers, it attempted to give a pan India news coverage for its readers. While remaining ambivalent towards colonial rule, much of its coverage of the events (and tragedies) concerning the trials and tribulations indicated that it's sympathies lay with the erstwhile Nawabi rule of Awadh. Today, the back issues provide valuable insight into the happenings in and around Lucknow, when the British were establishing their rule and tinkering with the socio-political milieu of the region in that hazy period between the annexation and the First War of Independence. The readership of *Tilism*, however, was not confined to Lucknow alone; the paper's popularity increased exponentially, with readership extending to a far-off place like Lahore. Moreover, the paper was read by a cross-section of society, ranging from erstwhile nobles of the decimated Nawabi court, Company officials, as well as common citizens.

Tilism's fearless accounts clearly indicate that resentment had started brewing among the common citizens against the high-handedness of even lowly Company officials; from the ruthless occupation of the royal palaces, the remodelling of Lucknow city, the local conflicts between landowners (*ta'alukdars* and *zamindars*), to the deleterious economic effects of Company policies - the newspaper covered all, boldly and in detail. The *Tilism* survived a mere 42 issues, it's last issue being dated May 8, 1857, the date around which the tragic events of 1857 engulfed the region. The editor, Mohammad Yakub, survived the insurrection and launched another newspaper, *Karnamah* in July 1865, which he continued to publish till his death in 1903.

Oudh (Awadh) Akhbar

Launched in 1859 by Munshi Nawal Kishore from his famous Nawal Kishore Press at Lucknow, the newspaper continued to be published for almost a century. It managed to fill a vacuum due to initial absence of local competition. Initially a four page weekly publication, its frequency gradually increased till it became a daily newspaper from 1877, being the first Urdu daily of northern India. *Awadh Akhbar*'s masthead depicted a sketch of the *Chattar Manzil / Farhat Baksh* palace complex, a spin-off from the colonial-era *Illustrated London News*. Publishing a wide gamut of news items, including international happenings, local social and cultural events, and serialising of Urdu fiction, the newspaper saw rapid change in its editors, as a consequence of which, its format, content and USP also kept varying.

Fig. 69: Masthead of *Awadh Akhbar.*

A number of factors contributed to the success of *Awadh Akhbar*; the first and foremost being the patronage that the press received from the colonial government, including advertisements and notifications. Also, unlike others of the genre, it was professionally managed and operated on sound commercial principles, although the initial issues of *Awadh Akhbar* were edited by *Munshi ji* himself. Maulvi Hadi Ali "Ashq" was the first formal editor of the newspaper, who was appointed in 1859, but left in 1864. One of the most prominent editors of *Awadh Akhbar* was Pandit Ratan Nath "Sarshar", who was appointed to this post in 1878. *Fasana-e-Azad*, a magnum opus Urdu novel by Sarshar was serialised in *Awadh Akhbar* from 1878 onwards, before it was published in four volumes by the Nawal Kishore Press. The story described a wandering character named Azad and his companion, Khoji, from the streets of late nineteenth century Lucknow to the battlefields of the Russo-Turkish War (1877–1878). Sarshar conceived of writing *Fasana-e-Azad* after the success of the articles he contributed to *Awadh Akhbar* under the heading *Zarafat* (wit and humour). His work was studied later by literary critics as the first Urdu novel and for its influence on the genre. More importantly, its colourful narration served as an important descriptive source for Lucknow, its people, and its culture, in those days.

Abdul Halim 'Sharar', later to be known as the "cultural biographer of Lucknow" also served as its assistant editor during 1880 - 1882. Sharar left later to concentrate on his own newspaper, *Dil Gudaz*. He was also involved in an unsavoury controversy with Pandit Braj Narayan "Chakbast" (discussed later in this Chapter). The debate spilled over in competing publications, *Dil Gudaz* and *Awadh Punch*. In 1919, the Nawal Kishore press even brought out a book on the debate, titled *Mubahasa-e-Gulzar-e- Nasim yani Masraka-e-Chakbast va Sharar.* The press would later receive acclaim over the publication of another magnum opus, *Tilism-e-Hoshruba*, by Munshi Ahmad Hussain Qarmar, translated by Mohammad Hussain Jah in the 1930s.

Despite being a commercial success in its heydays, and continued support from the colonial government, this very aspect of *Awadh Akhbar* contributed its decline later on. Seen as a mouth piece of the British, and unsupportive of the Indian National Congress, the newspaper (and the press) found itself on the wrong side of the freedom movement. By the 1890s, its popularity and circulation took a nosedive. Its content also suffered, as it seemed to be caught in a time warp, unable to appreciate the requirements of the day and the reading choice of its readers. However it managed to survive till 1950 even after India had gained Independence.

The Oudh Punch

Punch and Judy fought for a pie,
Punch gave Judy a knock in the eye.

Says Punch to Judy, "Will you have any more?"
Says Judy to Punch, "My eye is too sore."

The roots of the immensely popular glove puppet or marionette play, *Punch and Judy* seems to have had roots in Italy, way back from the 1660s. The show became much sought-after in Britain during the eighteenth century, as puppet shows caught on in fairs and puppet theatres. Punch metamorphosed into a hunch-backed, pot bellied surly character, who did not hesitate to use his stick on his wife, Judy, herself a shrew. The duo provided comic, satirical relief to the audience, complete with innuendoes, many topics dealing with marital discord. A British weekly magazine of satirical humour, *Punch* was launched in 1841 in London, when the concept of cartooning or more specifically, satirical cartooning, was in its formative years. In fact, the term "cartoon" was first used in *Punch* in 1843. The masthead of the magazine was based on the puppet character of Punch from *Punch and Judy*. *Punch* grew in popularity, with circulation breaching the 100,000 mark in 1910, going upto 184,000 during wartime. The publication of the magazine was finally closed down in 2002, after declining readership led to financial losses. Over a period of one and half centuries, it was obvious that readership preferences had changed, and lampooning political figures with snide cartoons and innuendoes was no longer considered humorous. Other avenues had opened up for this sport.

If London had its *Punch*, could colonial Lucknow be far behind? After noting the success of serio-comic newspapers of those times, one Mohammad Sajjad Hussain of Kakori, an alumnus of Canning College, set up a lithographic press in Golaganj, Lucknow and invited his friends to send him their contributions. January 16, 1877 saw the launch of the first issue of a weekly illustrated paper, *The Oudh Punch,* with eight pages. Initially, only 250 copies were printed, which later went up to 500 copies, each copy priced at four *annas*. Its pages were increased to 12 in number, with periodic supplements also. Initially, *The Oudh Punch* was looked upon with suspicion, both by fellow Indians was well as the colonial rulers, who suspected that it would be used as a means of propaganda, but their fears were unfounded. The magazine consisted more of social articles, poetry, songs and witty articles, including art, instead of containing any incendiary material. But it did not shy away from contemporary issues like communalism, British war efforts in Europe, Afghanistan and elsewhere and even transcribing and adapting selective articles and art from the original *Punch*, *Fun* and *The Graphic* of London. Artists for the publication included Ganga Sahai "Shauq" and a Wazir Ali. The local art was crude but evocative.

Fig. 70: Masthead of *The Oudh Punch.*

The contributors of *Oudh Punch* included Akbar Allahabadi, Pandit Ratan Nath Sarshar, Syed Mohammad Azad, Tribhavan Nath Hijr, and several others, who provided humorous and satirical content (poetry and prose) for the newspaper through several decades. The masthead of the newspaper was emblazoned with the motto, "Life is Pleasure", apparently inspired by an old proverb, signifying that unless we endeavour to be happy in life and enjoy it, it is better not to have lived at all. The main protagonist in the newspaper was often Mr (Oudh) Punch, while any number of characters could be incorporated in the narrative, including John Bull (the British government). An early plate of the newspaper, drawn by Ganga Sahai hilariously depicted Mr (Oudh) Punch sitting at the head of a table,

Fig. 71: A Literary Symposium, *The Oudh Punch.*

with an Englishman on his right hand, a Nawab on his left, together with a Sikh gentleman and a Maratha. Others in the group are a Muslim, a Bengali, a Parsee, a Jew and a Turk. The characteristic features of each nationality / community is cleverly depicted by way of appearance, particularly attire. Thus, the intent of the periodical was perfectly clear: to provide entertainment, through wit, satire, jest and caricature. In the process, it did not hesitate to lampoon British officials and personalities.

One of the reasons (out of many) for the success of the newspaper was its easy availability. Home delivery was free to any address at Lucknow, but additional subscription and postal charges were levied for delivery in the United Kingdom. It was even sent to Burma and member countries under the Postal Union! Sajjad Hussain himself donned the multiple roles of Proprietor, Editor and Publisher. Inspired by the success of *The Oudh Punch*, illustrated papers such as *The Indian Punch* (Lucknow), *The Delhi Punch* and *The Punjab Punch* (both from Lahore) and similar publications from Bombay, Madras and Calcutta also emerged, but later sank without a trace.

Contrary to its initial political stand, *The Oudh Punch* later became increasingly critical of British rule and was closed down in 1912; however, it was again revived in 1916. The last edition of *The Oudh Punch* was printed in December 1937.

Dil Gudaz

In 1886, Sharar was advised by Maulvi Bashir-ud-Din (of *Al Bashir*) and Munshi Nisar Hussain (of *Payam-e-Yar*) to start a publication devoted to literature and history. January 1887 saw the launching of *Dil Gudaz* - a publication which had such a chequered record and publication history that is quite a task to document it. Originally costing one rupee, its price was increased to two rupees and a serialised historical novel was provided as a free supplement. It gained popularity by leaps and bounds, but did not provide a steady income for its owner. In 1891, due to financial constraints, Sharar stopped the publication of the paper and proceeded to Hyderabad to join the services of Nawab Wiqar-ul-Umra. 1893 saw Sharar requesting a friend to resume the publication of *Dil Gudaz* from Lucknow, but it faced resistance, due to the content of some of its articles, and the paper ceased publication once again, with Sharar proceeding to England in 1893, on an assignment of the Nawab. He returned to Hyderabad in 1896, and resumed the publication of *Dil Gudaz* from 1898.

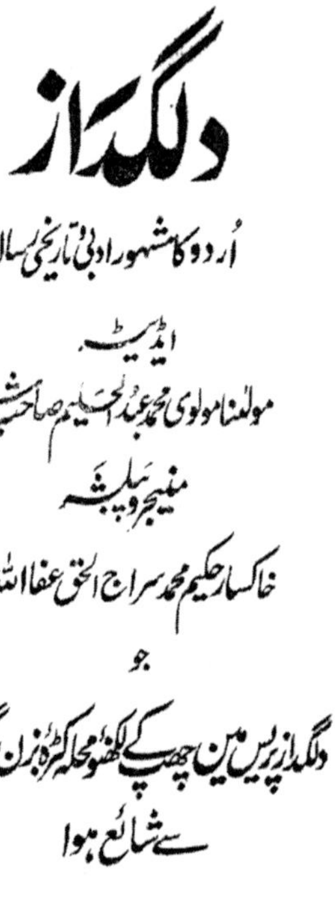

دلگداز

اُردو کا مشہور ادبی و تاریخی رسالہ

ایڈیٹر

مولنا مولوی محمد عبد الحلیم صاحب شرر

منیجر و پبلشر

خاکسار حکیم محمد سراج الحق عفا اللہ عنہ

جو

دلگداز پریس مین چھپ کے لکھنؤ محلہ کٹرہ بزن بیگ خان

سے شائع ہوا

Fig. 72: Abdul Halim Sharar's *Dil Gudaz*.

With history repeating itself once again and the contents of the paper being challenged by Muslim orthodoxy, Sharar was compelled to leave Hyderabad with the newspaper also getting relocated to its origins, i.e. Lucknow. In 1901, Sharar once again tried for an assignment in Hyderabad, and the periodical remained in suspended animation from 1901 - 1904, after which, Sharar returned to Lucknow and resumed its publication. The paper always provided serialised Urdu novels as supplements; indeed in this manner, it can be said that The *Oudh Punch* and *Dil Gudaz* rendered the same service to the Urdu novel as the *Tatler* and the *Spectator* did for the English novel. In 1908, *Dil Gudaz* was published from Hyderabad, as Sharar accepted the post of Assistant Director of Education in the state, but was temporarily suspended, when Sharar left once again for Lucknow and resuscitated *Dil Gudaz* in 1910.

بسم اللہ الرحمن الرحیم

ہندوستان مین مشرقی تمدن کا آخری نمونہ

یعنی گذشتہ لکھنؤ

(۱)

اس کے تسلیم کرنے مین شاید کسی کو عذر نہ ہوگا کہ ہندوستان مین مشرقی تہذیب
تمدن کا جو آخری نمونہ نظر آیا وہ گذشتہ دربار اودھ تھا۔ اگلے دور کی یادگار
اور بھی کئی دربار موجود ہین مگر جس دربار پر پرانی تہذیب اور اگلی معاشرت کا
خاتمہ ہوگیا۔ وہ یہی دربار تھا۔ جو بہت ہی آخر مین قائم ہوا اور عجیب و غریب
ترقیان دکھا کے بہت ہی جلد فنا ہوگیا۔ لہذا مندرجہ بالا عنوان کے تحت مین ہم
اس مرحوم دربار کے مختصر حالات اور اُس کی خصوصیتون کو بیان کرنا چاہتے ہین
اسکے تسلیم کرنے مین بھی شاید کسی کو عذر نہ ہوگا کہ جس خطۂ زمین پر پچھلا دربار
قائم ہوا اُس کی وقعت اور اہمیت ہندوستان کے تمام صوبون سے بڑھی ہوئی ہے۔
پُرانے چندربنسی خاندان خصوصاً راجہ رامچندر جی کے اعلیٰ کارنامے اور عدیم النظیر
ناموریان اس درجۂ کمال کو پہونچی ہوئی ہین کہ تاریخ کے ظرف کو تنگ اور محدود دیکھ
کے اُنھون نے مذہبی تقدس کا جامہ پہن لیا ہے۔ اور آج ہندوستان کا شاید ہی
کوئی ایسا بدنصیب گاؤن ہوگا جہان اُنکی یاد ہر سال رام لیلا کے مذہبی ناٹک کے
ذریعے سے تازہ نہ کرلی جاتی ہو۔ لیکن اودھ کے اُس قدیم ترین دیوتائی دربار کے
حالات اور اجودھیا کا اُس عہد کا جاہ و جلال والمیکی نے ایسی معجزنما فصاحت
کے ساتھ دکھایا کہ وہ ہر عقیدت کیش کی لوح دل پر کُھد گیا۔ لہذا ہمین اُسکے اعادے
کی ضرورت نہین۔ جن لوگون نے اجودھیا کے اُس زمانے کی تصویر والمیکی کے لٹریری
مرقع مین دیکھی ہے وہ اُسی مبارک خطے پر آج دلگداز مین فیض آباد کی تصویر دیکھین
لہذا ہم سلسلۂ واقعات کو اُس وقت سے شروع کرتے ہین جب اس آخری دربار کی
بنیاد پڑی جسے فنا ہوئے کچھ اوپر پچاس سال سے زیادہ زمانہ نہین ہوا۔
جب نواب برہان الملک امین الدین خان نیشاپوری شہنشاہی دربار دہلی

Fig. 73: *Hindustan Mein Mashriqui Tamaddun ka Akhri Namuna.*

Over a period of several decades, *Dil Gudaz* also saw changes in its format, subscription cost, number of pages and content. Serialisation of Sharar's own novels in the newspaper compelled an increase in the number of pages and well as cost. Starting from being a sixteen page monthly periodical, by 1906, it had become a voluminous magazine consisting of fifty six pages. The page size was also enlarged with increased size of lettering (font size in today's jargon). In his writings, Sharar remained critical of the more regressive aspects of Islam, e.g. the *purdah* (veil) system for Muslim ladies; he also did not spare Christian practices, which earned him many detractors and critics. The writer felt that the Indian National Congress, then a potent force in the National Movement, was doing more harm than good towards Hindu Muslim unity. He seemed to have realised late in life that *Dil Gudaz* was excessively Islam oriented and to correct this shortcoming, he invited Hindu friends to contribute to his journal, so that it became truly multi-cultural, without any religious biases.

However, today Sharar is best known for his articles on the lost culture and heritage of Lucknow which he wrote as a series of articles called *Hindustan Mein Mashriqui Tamaddun ka Akhri Namuna* in *Dil Gudaz* from 1913 onwards. His own compilation, *Mazamin-e-Sharar* published from Lahore, contained many of these articles. Sharar described the history of Lucknow as well as the lifestyle of its people, including their religion, education, medicine, ceremonies and etiquette, dress, culinary arts, calligraphy, entertainment and pastimes. Abdul Halim "Sharar" died in Lucknow on Dec 1, 1926. By all accounts, *Dil Gudaz* continued beyond his death to as late as 1929, under the tutelage of his son.

A Literary Feud

Of Kashmiri origin, Pandit Brij Narayan Chakbast was born in 1882 at Faizabad. His family shifted to Lucknow in 1887 and started residing in *Kashmiri Mohalla* of old Lucknow. Brij Narayan completed his education, obtaining a degree in law and started practicing law in Lucknow. He became popular as a *nazm* poet of the Lucknow school of poetry, being strongly influenced by Mirza Ghalib, Mir Anis and Khwaja Haider Ali Atish "Lakhnawi." Braj Narayan also participated in the freedom movement, and was actively involved in social and political movements of his time. He would organise all India *mushairas* (social gatherings in evenings where Urdu poetry was recited, typically taking the form of a contest) annually, and also initiated and participated in community development programmes target towards Kashmiri youth. Chakbast's patriotic fervour found its finest expression in his elegies on the deaths of national leaders, e.g. Bal Gangadhar Tilak. Chakbast also dedicated a poem to Mahatma Gandhi who was still working in South Africa at the time.

In 1905, Chakbast published an edition of a *masnavi* (Arabic: *mathnawī* or Persian: *masnavi* - a kind of poem written in rhyming couplets, or more specifically "a poem based on independent, internally rhyming lines" on the Sufi tradition) called *Gulzar-e-Nasim* by Pandit Daya Shankar Kaul "Nasim." Sharar responded vehemently against this in *Dil Gudaz*, with other writers and editors taking sides. It appeared that Sharar was trying to exclude the "Kashmiri" element from chaste Urdu literature, which he felt should be confined to Lucknow and nearby areas. In that era, where ethnic, linguistic and religious identities were assuming more and more importance during colonial rule, this rivalry soon spread wide, with writers and printing presses from Kanpur and even Hyderabad joining in the fray. In fact, this state of affairs indicated the identity crisis among the Urdu speaking masses, particularly those involved in literary pursuits. The contestations were further fuelled by the unfortunate fact that imperialism was rapidly establishing roots in the new world order and local litterateurs were at best second class citizens. From open, verbal debates and oral communication, the printed word was easier to disseminate and a person could now express his views from the confines of his home, so to say. The *Awadh Akhbar* chose to stay away from the controversy, but the *Awadh Punch* remained in the forefront of this debate. Young Chakbast gained a certain amount of notoriety in this whole episode, due to his debate and confrontation with Sharar, a much senior and distinguished writer and journalist during that period. In 1913, Mirzā Muḥammad Shafī' Shirāzī collected sixty articles that dealt with the controversy between Sharar and Chakbast regarding Nasīm's *Gulzar-e-Nasim*, and published it as *Mubāḥiṡa-e-Gulzār-e Nasīm ya'nī Ma'raka-e-Chakbast o Sharar* under the auspices of the Nawal Kishore press, Lucknow.

One of the fall-outs of this unfortunate controversy between the veteran Sharar and the youthful Chakbast was that as the debate got more and more acrimonious, many personal skeletons started emerging from cupboards. Sharar, who had been a highly respected journalist and author was at the receiving end of all this. Sajjad Hussain of *Awadh Punch* wrote deprecatingly of Sharar, labelling him as a writer who was "easily able to create historical events about which it is impossible to find historical witness, but his *ḳhāyāl* ["imagination"] was so strong that it was not difficult to create strange and wondrous events in this head of his." Sharar had tried to advance the premise that the *masnavi* in question was the work of Atish, and simultaneously, it also fell short of the language of Lucknow. Thus, Sharar's faulty logic not only downplayed Chakbast and Nasim - according to him, Atish had also failed to express himself in the *Lakhnavi andaz* in the debated *masnavi.* In those days, Sheikh Imam Baksh "Nasikh" and Khwaja Haider Ali "Atish" were considered to be the founders of the Lucknow school of poetry. Thus, Sharar's wild allegations were unacceptable to the public and dismissed as a mere figment of his imagination.

Awadh Punch, being a journal devoted to satire, took this opportunity to lampoon Sharar, drawing upon his roots in Kursi (an area then in the outskirts of Lucknow, infamous for its slow-witted inhabitants). However, Sharar was not without his supporters, prominent among whom were Hakim Barham and Riyaz Khairabadi of *Riyaz-ul-Akbar*. Till now Sharar had been known for his respectable lineage in the erstwhile Nawabi court, both at Lucknow and Metia Burz, Calcutta, as well as his connections in the state of Hyderabad. His writings had earned him fame and respectability. But with disclosures about his rustic origins and propensity to write in hyperbole, even his description of Lucknow's erstwhile Nawabi court and the Lucknow way of life, which had become a sort of chronicle for Lucknow's lost heritage became debatable and open to question. Today, Sharar is best known for his series of articles on Lucknow, published in *Dil Gudaz*, titled *Hindustan Mein Mashriqi Tamaddun Ka Akhri Namuna* or *Guzista Lakhnau*, in which he described the history of Lucknow as well as the lifestyle of its people, including their religion, education, medicine, ceremonies and etiquette, dress, culinary arts, calligraphy, entertainment and pastimes. These articles were later translated into

English and compiled into a single volume called *Lucknow: The Last Phase of an Oriental Culture*. This effectively earned him the honour of being recognised as the cultural biographer of Lucknow, although Sharar had neither personally observed nor lived through the *Lakhnavi* experience, which he detailed so passionately. Sadly, in present times, on reading the narrative and observations of his detractors above, one is compelled to ponder as to how much of Sharar's narrative on the lost heritage of Lucknow was authentic, and how much was overstatement and exaggeration.

NIGHTMARE AT *FIRAQ MANZIL* - A NOVELLA

I

2020

As one enters Lucknow's *Chowk* area through the derelict *Gol Darwaza*, one's senses are assailed by a myriad of sights, smells and crowds, as people go about their daily routine in this old area of the city. The *Darwaza* or gateway has a chequered history, presumably built during the times Asaf-ud-Daula, the famed Nawab of Awadh. *Chowk* itself has undergone changes since it came into existence, more than two and half centuries ago. Many of the old *kothis* with *dyodhies* (traditional mansions with porches) have been torn down either partially or completely, to be replaced by garish shops and elevated showrooms equipped with marble-lined steps and shiny steel fittings, selling mostly items of clothing, jewellery and groceries. Here and there, one can see remnants of old buildings, shanties and narrow dingy lanes, veering off from both sides into the interiors of the area. The sight can be intimidating for the uninitiated.

One such lane, about two hundred meters from the gateway, on the right side, is expectedly narrow in the beginning, but widens somewhat, as one proceeds further down. At the entrance of the lane, an ancient old man, accompanied by a young boy, possibly his grandson, sits in a tiny wooden stall selling wilted flowers. His rheumy eyes and frail constitution can be deceptive; he possesses a powerful, stentorious voice and has a lucid knowledge of the area. He willingly and intelligibly explains the way to *Firaq Manzil*, which is situated further down in this side lane. However, no vehicle, not even a *rickshaw,* can enter into the narrow stretch. One has to leave his means of transport and walk down to his destination - there being no other alternative. The lane meanders, with derelict homes on either side, having low wooden doors, the wood having long gone to seed. Shallow pools of dirty water, on either side of the lane, small heaps of garbage, few prancing goats and an occasional public tap with urchins frolicking in the gushing water, do not inspire confidence.

For a person who is not conversant with the traditional private dwellings of the city from the Nawabi period, the area resembles a jumble of disorganised structures, more like cubby holes than mansions. But outward appearances are often delusory. For many of these low arches, with crumbling wooden doors, lead to former spacious residences inside, with open courtyards, *mardana* and *zenana* structures and quite possibly a personal *Imambara*. *Firaq Manzil* is one such rambling place, approachable by an elevated path leading to a gateway, which has all but toppled, but its pillars standing strong. On entering, one sees a moderately large open quadrangle, paved with stones, low roofed, colonnaded buildings on either side of the open space and an *Imambara* in front. The latter place of worship and congregation is better maintained than the wings on either side. However, there is nothing ostentatious. The buildings are crudely painted with lime wash in typical *Lakhnavi* style, with few steps leading to squat pillared verandahs and high roofs. The doorways have typical Adam-style fanlights, equipped with colored glass. The left side building or eastern wing, seems to be neglected and decayed. Cobwebs hang around in the corners; tiny clumps of vegetation can be seen in the spaces between the paving and on the parapet. There is a general air of dissipation and lack of human activity. The servants' quarters, kitchens, water well, sheds and outhouses behind the main buildings cannot be observed from the front. In general, *Firaq Manzil* is just another old *kothi* with a *dyodhi*, among scores of others in the area. It is not a setting for something out of nightmares. So when a nightmarish horror came, it was unexpected and its forces were doubled.

2010

Fatima Nasreen had met Yusuf in Aligarh Muslim University

when both were science major students; it was love at first sight. Fatima was a slight girl, moderately attractive, short-statured, with prominent crinkly hair, which she hated and tried to unsuccessfully straighten out with the usual electrical devices and by frequent visits to a dingy beauty parlour near the University gate. Yusuf was tall and broad-shouldered, his most prominent feature being an unruly shock of hair which fell over his left eye. Studious by nature, he avoided out-door activities, but fate would later make him enter a profession where he would be outdoors, in dense forests, all through his lifetime. He was enamoured by Fatima's crinkly hair, and failed to understand her anathema towards something so attractive.

Their romance had been prolonged and tedious. Prolonged, because they had accepted their situation with equanimity, knowing fully well that marriage was out of question until Yusuf acquired a stable job. It had been tedious because Fatima's parents, both of whom were practicing doctors in old Delhi, were in no mood to let their only daughter waste her life over a student graduating in science - when there were reasonably good offers for her *nikah*, as soon as she completed her graduation. Fatima had been unable to fulfil her parents' aspirations and become a doctor herself. And now she had this unwanted romance at Aligarh. But she managed to get her way and join Masters in Botany, with Yusuf joining likewise. Yusuf drew his lineage from the old families of Lucknow and Rampur. But now, other than the lineage, nothing much remained, especially family wealth. But the youth, who had a serious bent of mind, was already preparing earnestly for the Indian Forest Service examination. This, he felt, would be comparatively easier to crack, than the tougher CSE, also conducted by the UPSC. The waiting was tiresome for both of them; indeed at some point of time, the young couple had even thought of going their separate ways. But fate intervened and Yusuf was selected in the Indian Forest Service within two years. Things looked promising at last, but there were many unforeseen hurdles yet to appear.

2015

Yusuf's in-service training took him to Dehra Dun, and luckily or unluckily, he was allotted Uttarakhand cadre. He was lucky because at least he was nearer to his home state, as compared to his batch mates, some of whom were posted in the forests of Naxal-infested Jharkhand, or Tamil Nadu and Karnataka, the latter by now famous for their poachers and sandal-wood smugglers. Although Uttarakhand had no law and order problems, yet he was unlucky because the state's topography was unfriendly, 86 percent being mountainous and 65 percent covered by dense forests, many areas being extremely isolated, unapproachable, quite a few being above the snow line in winters. Accepting Yusuf's now elite status, Fatima's parents got her married to the young IFS officer in a low-key wedding ceremony, since Yusuf's parents were long dead and few of his surviving relatives, including a distant uncle in Rampur, were not in favour of anything extravagant or pretentious. A young entrant, Yusuf hardly had any accumulated leave in his service account, and could not afford to go for a prolonged honeymoon. After spending three days of leisure at Mussoorie, he hurriedly re-joined duty at Almora, with Fatima in tow. A beautiful colonial-era cottage, now functioning as the Forest Office rest house at Khagmara, served as their temporary abode.

"Fatima, have you thought how we shall manage, when I have to report for duty in the interiors of the state?" asked Yusuf suddenly, his eyebrows frowning. They were enjoying a simple dinner served by the guesthouse cook-cum-*chowkidar*, before retiring to bed.

"Why, can't I accompany you? Won't there be official quarters allotted to you?" Fatima responded innocently.

"That is OK, but some of these forests are really dense, with risk of wild animal attack. Also, the quarters are not exactly models of luxury. In fact, they are rustic and quite primitive in many places," replied Yusuf with a worried look, as the realisation suddenly hit him. "I do not want luxury, dear," replied Fatima, "I just want to be with you and take care of your needs while you are busy with your day-to-day routine."

But now, this nagging worry took hold of Yusuf. He had no illusions of leading a comfortable domestic life, once he had assumed his charge in some isolated outpost, surrounded by deep forests, possibly infested by wild animals. He was prepared to survive with bare minimum facilities and eat basic food prepared in a desultory manner by some staff of the camp, but what would happen to his young city bred wife? And God forbid, if there was some medical emergency? How could they raise a family in due course of time, unless he could manage a posting in some district headquarters, if not in Dehra Dun itself? Sensing that it would be futile to trouble Fatima with such troublesome thoughts, he finished his dinner quietly and prepared to retire to bed. But his young wife was no fool; neither was she unaware of the situation. She decided to avoid the topic for the moment and pursue the matter later. The day ended on a disappointing note for both.

2020

"Ammi, Ammi, look at me!" yelled Tahira, a doll-like child, barely three years of age, as she balanced herself precariously on the branch of a large tree in the forest department camp, near to the official quarters of Yusuf. Much water had flowed down the Alaknanda since the conversation of Yusuf and Fatima above. His postings had not proved to be so perilous after all, which had encouraged him to raise his family among the rustic surroundings. Other families in the camp formed a close-knit community and help was always at hand. Fatima smiled at her daughter, knowing fully well that the child faced no risk - she could clamber up trees without a second thought and engage in all sorts of tomboyish activities; after all, she was not city bred - she was a doughty child, born and brought up in natural surroundings, among tall coniferous trees in verdant valleys. The child attended a pre-nursery "school" in the camp itself, and led a carefree, happy life.

Yusuf's ramshackle jeep entered the residential area, and he hurriedly got down, reaching his living quarters with long strides. Throwing a smile at the giggling Tahira, he entered his home and beckoned to Fatima to come inside. His wife was quick to note that her husband was tense and worried.

"What's the matter, dear?" she asked.

"The news is not good, Fatima," replied Yusuf with a frown. "Do you remember Rajive Malhotra, a young DFO, whom we had met during Diwali gathering last year?"

"Yes, somewhat," responded Fatima. "But what happened?"

"Well, he has been badly mauled by a leopard during one of his patrols, and is being rushed to Dehra. His survival is doubtful."

"Allah!! I pray that he should recover and live a long life," said Fatima.

"But the worst is yet to come, dear," exclaimed Yusuf. "I am being relieved to take over his charge immediately, as there is no officer of equivalent rank at hand."

"Is it so bad, Yusuf?" asked Fatima innocently.

"Well, good and bad, I cannot say, but the posting has a nasty reputation for sure," Yusuf replied. "The area is overrun with wild animals, and there is not much the Forest Department staff can do, equipped as they are with batons and nets. Guns, of course are not allowed, except in dire emergencies. And anyway, the guns are outdated and obsolete. Also...." and here, Yusuf stopped at mid-sentence.

"Also what?"

"The area has human habitations in three to four scattered villages, but these people do not like outsiders like us. Moreover, they are reputed to be practitioners of all sorts of black arts, including magic, sacrifice and worship of earth spirits for casting spells. We do not disturb them and they do not disturb us, although we are aware that they surreptitiously trap protected animals, nor for eating but for practicing magic. The community is known as *Kallu Pahari* and is shunned by other communities living in nearby villages."

"I really don't know how to respond to this, Yusuf," frowned Fatima. "In fact, I am a bit surprised that you can believe this mumbo-jumbo in this day and age."

"You belong to Delhi, Fatima," replied Yusuf gently. "You are a city-bred girl who does not understand these things. I lost my parents at a young age and grew up in a village in Rampur district, being looked after by my uncle's family. They preferred to lead a simple village life, although we had substantial ancestral property in old Lucknow. The property was reported to be cursed by an evil entity, or entities, I do not know. But I do know that the curse did not let my uncle live in peace even in his village. Misfortune and unexplainable tragic events followed him and his family throughout his life, and continues to do so even now."

"You mean that this entity or spirit or whatever, was determined to make your uncle's life a misery, wherever he went? But why?" Fatima eyes grew round at this revelation.

"I have no idea, dear," replied Yusuf tersely. "But I had thought I would be free of these things as I grew up and settled far away from family ties. But it seems, I shall face a similar problem in Rikiyasain, the land of the *Kallu Pahari.*"

"Why so?"

"Because apparently Rajive had caught the villagers trying to sacrifice a sloth bear, under a tree, having a makeshift image, after beating the poor creature half dead with sticks. Rajive had confiscated the "sacrifice" and warned the wrong-doers using strong language. In response, the headman, a ruffian called Chander Rawat, had warned Rajive that he would be dead within 24 hours due to his blasphemy. And now this poor officer is fighting for his life!!"

Both Yusuf and Fatima fell silent after this discussion, each lost in his / her thoughts. Fatima did not entirely disbelieve Yusuf's story of the supernatural, although she felt that the leopard attack could be a mere coincidence. Fatima was a rational woman with an open mind. She was aware that science could not explain many phenomena, and ghostly activity was one such area where science had not been able to make much headway. This did not mean that the supernatural did not exist. Most probably it did. It was alright as long as it did not turn malevolent and harmful, so she felt.

"Fatima, although you can stay in these quarters for some time, we would have to vacate it in due course, and you will have to join me in my place of posting," muttered Yusuf. "We have a young child and her education is just starting. We cannot keep her in such an isolated place at this stage."

"So what do you suggest?"

"I have been wracking my brains on the problem, ever since I came to know about the situation," Yusuf responded. "An option would be to send you to Lucknow, with Tahira. My ancestral property is lying vacant there. You can live there comfortably, as the opposite wing is occupied by my cousin brothers and their families. They would help you set up an establishment. Also Tahira would get far better education in Lucknow, than she would have in this remote area."

Fatima's heart fluttered with anxiety as the realisation hit her. Her life and her daughter's future were suddenly on the cross-roads. Harsh decisions had to be taken; her life was about to change and she would have to live without her husband.

"And what about you, Yusuf?" she enquired.

"I will join of course. No option there. But I will get a joining period leave, which I will use to drop you at Lucknow and help you settle there. Then I will return here," Yusuf replied.

Fatima had never been to Lucknow, although she had heard a lot about this famed Nawabi city and its unique laid-back culture. She was excited to be able to live in this city, but alone? What would her life be like? And she had a young daughter to take care of. But she possessed grit and determination, and would not let her emotions and insecurities come in the way of her domestic life. Her husband needed her support; after all they had married, fully knowing about the uncertainties that his job entailed. What would be the point of creating issues now? She, therefore, agreed to Yusuf's proposal, her mind already busy, planning about her impending journey and a new life-style that was fast approaching her.

II

The British-era Doon Express chugged into Lucknow's colonial *Charbagh* railway station sharply at 8.30 am. It was a crisp March morning. Yusuf and his family got down hurriedly from the train; their journey had been comfortable and they were raring to start a new life, far removed from forests, animals and practitioners of the black art.

"Yusuf, is it true that this train has been running on this route for more than a century now?" Fatima asked innocently.

"Possibly yes, but I can't be sure, Fatima," replied Yusuf, his mind already busy with future plans and a hundred other details one is usually confronted with, in a transfer and posting.

Their cab plunged into the crowded roads of Lucknow, heading swiftly towards the old quarter of the city. The milling crowds and traffic did not intimidate Fatima - after all, she herself was a product of old Delhi. But their young daughter seemed speechless on seeing throngs of people for the first time in her young life. Her carefree existence among tall trees, vast open spaces and fresh air suddenly seemed far away. The crowds, bright shops and tall buildings seemed exciting, but the air was stale and smog was everywhere, which made the child cough. Things would never be the same again for her.

Their approach to *Firaq Manzil* was intimidating, as they had to half carry and half drag their luggage, while walking up the winding lane. Once inside, they were greeted by Shoeb and Akhtar, cousins of Yusuf, who now lived with their families, in the right wing of the rambling house. Shoeb's wife, Faiza, and Kausar who was Akhtar's better half, embraced Fatima and led her inside their dwelling. Their two children, Salima and Adil, almost the same age as that of Tahira, danced around their cousin. The children were elated that they had got a new playmate. Tahira stood silently, her innocent mind absorbing the new atmosphere of this huge house with its high ceiling, arched walls and a somewhat gloomy atmosphere. The extended family gathered around a substantial breakfast, after which the nitty-gritty of Fatima occupying the left wing with her daughter was discussed.

"Yusuf, your portion of the house is vacant and it has four large rooms, including the original *dewan khana* (sitting room), as well as a huge *bawarchi khana* (kitchen) and two *ghusal khane* (washrooms). At best you can use two rooms as living and bedrooms. The other rooms can remain locked as they are. After all, it is very difficult to clean and maintain such a huge premises, when you are alone with your young child," suggested Shoeb. Yusuf nodded in agreement, but Fatima wanted to see the entire wing, before taking any decision. The cousins had managed to clean the rooms and washrooms, on their own, but the huge verandah was still dusty, with vegetation growing between the stone paving. It would take a lot of effort to make the wing spick and span, and even more effort and money to keep it that way. The kitchen was huge and dark, but with renovation and proper fittings, it would not be so intimidating. Yusuf would spent a week putting things ship-shape, aided by his cousins. An old lady from the neighbourhood had been roped in to act as a maid. An aged and decrepit gardener, who occasionally made an appearance in the property, would clean the paving, and install some potted plants in the premises.

Fatima decided to use three of the rooms - one of the rooms, the original *dewan khana* would be a nursery and playroom for Tahira. Her daughter was not used to enclosed spaces, and would be happier to have her own large den, in her own private world of dolls, story books and toys. The remaining last room would remain locked. On hearing Fatima's decision, Yusuf's cousins exchanged looks, but remained silent. For the next six days, carpenters, plumbers, electricians and workmen worked busily, giving the neglected wing a bright, cheerful and contemporary appearance. Yusuf had all but emptied his meagre savings bank account to pay for the work being done, as he wanted his wife and child to be comfortable and not feel deprived in any manner. After the renovation work was over, it was obvious that maximum effort and expense had been showered on Tahira's playroom. Originally this room had been the living room or *dewan khana* of *Firaq Manzil*, appropriately equipped with heavy furniture and furnishings to accommodate visitors and guests. Now the entire room was done up with pink shaded wood-work, matching contemporary fittings, including the storage spaces, with even the ceiling fan having Disney characters painted on it's wings. It had been transformed into a little girl's room - Yusuf made sure that Tahira would not feel any pangs of depression or deprivation, on being suddenly transposed from a happy-go-lucky life to a cloistered one in a rambling old house with unpleasant memories and associations. But even Yusuf was not very well conversant with whatever ill-association the house retained within itself. He had never lived here; he was only aware of he had been told by his uncle, and his memory was hazy. Maybe it was all superstition, perhaps it was all imagination, so he reasoned with himself, as he left for the railway station to board the Doon Express once again at night. But this time he was alone. His family was safely in Lucknow, in a house done up as best as possible, under the protection of his cousins, who were staying barely an arm's length away. All was well and under control.

Yusuf had not been informed that his colleague, Rajive had breathed his last in a government hospital in Dehra, due to blood toxaemia and septicaemia, caused by his fatal injuries. He had died within twenty fours after his confrontation with the village headman, Chander Rawat, as predicted by the latter.

It did not take long for Tahira to adjust to her new surroundings. She had not yet been admitted in a formal nursery school, and her time was spent in playing with her cousins. She especially loved to play hide-and-seek in the sprawling premises, with plenty of shadowy nooks and crannies. The huge well at the back of the house fascinated her, but unfortunately, it was boarded up and she could not peep inside. However, Tahira's favourite place soon became her own den, where she would spend hours, playing with her dolls, crooning to them as if they were alive. Within a few weeks, she withdraw from her boisterous games with her cousins and seemed to be content in her own company. This development disturbed Fatima slightly, but she kept quiet. Anyway, busy as she was in setting up her new establishment in a completely unknown city, which included Tahira's admission in a reputed school, she could hardly spend time worrying about her child's fascination for her den. After all, that had been the very purpose of providing the den to Tahira, was it not? In whatever spare time she had, Fatima, accompanied by one sister-in-law or the other, delightedly explored the famed markets of Lucknow and visited few of the better known monuments of the city, including the Residency and the *Bada Imambara.*

Tahira had always been a precocious child. Now, she seemed to derive a particular satisfaction of being alone in her den, even when her mother or her aunts were nearby. Tahira never felt lonely or scared. In fact, she felt secure, under the watchful protection of loving eyes, something which she did not feel even in her mother's presence. While sitting cross-legged on the floor, occupied with her toys, the child could occasionally sense a strange fragrance wafting near her; sometimes she felt that she had a playmate; however, this playmate was not another child, but someone older, a grown-up, like her mother. In her child-like innocence, once she even offered her toys to this "friend" whom she could not see, but of course, there had been no response. As the days passed, Tahira became more and more aware of the presence near her. She felt loved and protected, but she could never see anything, although she could recognise when the presence was nearby and when it was not. Her child-like logic told her that it was useless to tell her mother about these feelings. In any case, adults just could not understand the problems and feelings of little children, so she reasoned. Had her father been present, perhaps she would have ventured to discuss her experiences with him, but her mother was always busy, either with household work, gossiping with her sisters-in law, or exploring the city. Fatima had started to happily imbibe the Lucknow "feel" and was convinced that her daughter had adjusted marvellously well in her new, if somewhat cloistered surroundings. Of course, all these were only superficial, and there was much more to come.

Back in Rikiyasain, Yusuf was struggling to adjust himself to his new place of posting. This was the first time that he was separated from his family. This was also the first time that he was in a remote location, with hardly any outside contact. His living quarters were pitiable, and the enormity of his decision to join the Forest Services dawned upon him. Earlier, the news of his colleague's tragic death had stunned him. Yusuf's days were dreary and his nights lonely. Suddenly, life seemed to be a burden. Fortunately, he had not come across any member from the dreaded community that the area was infamous for. In any case, it was not their wherewithal to interact with outsiders or disturb them in any manner. They only seemed to react when thwarted or prevented from carrying out their day-to-day activities.

It was a warm sultry April afternoon, when Yusuf had a strange experience during his routine movement in the deep jungles of Rikiyasain. Earlier, he had received reports that a Himalayan black bear had been marauding the area, carrying off livestock but avoiding humans. As his jeep moved through the broken jungle path, shaking and careening, he spotted five or six locals running hither and thither, shouting hoarsely and waving sticks in the air. Obviously, the rampaging bear was nearby. Within few moments, the entire group disappeared among the trees, the forest being so dense in parts that it appeared to be quite dark, almost twilight. In his bid to prevent the jeep from running over the villagers, Yusuf's driver slammed on his brakes; the overheated engine sputtered and died. Yusuf and his team were suddenly stranded in the deep forest with a breakdown. His staff were unperturbed and one opened the bonnet to see the cause of overheating, while others examined the tyres and brakes to see if any serious damage had occurred. For them, it was part of a regular routine. In the meantime, Yusuf's eyes had adjusted to the dim light, and he fancied that he could see a human figure among the trees. He decided to approach the person and ask for directions, as it appeared that the person was actually wanting to talk to him, but away from the others.

Coming nearer, he could see a middle aged man, in typical Garhwali clothes, standing quietly among the shadows, waiting for Yusuf to be at arm's length. Despite his shabby attire and unkept appearance, he had piercing eyes and a commanding personality. Speaking in chaste Hindi, he asked Yusuf, "So you have come to replace Rajive saheb, who insulted us and our Gods?" Yusuf was flabbergasted. In a remote place like this, where everyone either spoke Garhwali or Hindi with a heavy accent, who could be this man speak in unaffected Hindi of the plains? And how did he know about his deceased colleague, Rajive?

The stranger continued, "Saheb, you are a long way off from the plains and your own home. Your wife and child are in danger. Try to save them before it's too late."

"Whhat.. what.. who are you? How do you know all this?" stammered Yusuf.

"That is not important, Saheb. I have no quarrel with you. Our people just want to live peacefully, continuing our old traditions and customs. Our Gods do not forgive anybody who blasphemes against them, or tries to disturb us in any way," replied the man, speaking softly, yet menacingly.

"But how do you know about my personal life?" persisted Yusuf.

"These eyes see all; these ears hear all, Saheb," the stranger answered. "I did not curse your friend. I did not cause him to die.

He insulted our Gods and brought the curse upon himself. I merely predicted what would happen to him due to the curse."

Yusuf remained tongue-tied before the forceful personality of this man from the deep jungles. He had this mental picture of a rustic brute, who had in some mysterious way caused the death of his colleague. But this man in front of him was no ruffian or trouble-maker. He looked sane, sober and his personality was indeed remarkable.

"I take your leave now, Saheb," continued the mysterious stranger, whom Yusuf could now identify as Chander Rawat. "But wait," the stranger paused, "As a measure of my goodwill, I give you this holy ash. Scatter it in four directions in your home. You might be protected from the evil that stalks you by day and watches you by night. I can say no more."

With these words, Rawat retraced his steps and soon vanished into the gloom of the forest. Yusuf was left standing flabbergasted, holding a small bag tied with string, which Rawat had given him before leaving.

That night, Yusuf could not sleep. He tossed and turned, his mind in a whirl, as he tried to weigh the options before him. There was no way that he could abandon his posting and rush off to Lucknow, on an imaginary or perceived threat - that too supernatural in nature. But the welfare of his young wife and child was foremost in his thoughts. How could he solve this problem, if at all there was a problem? Suddenly he remembered the charm that Chander had presented him. Could the bag be sent to his family if he could not go himself? But how? There were no courier services in the vicinity. He would have to approach his colleagues, identify someone who was proceeding to any town nearby and hand over the bag to him, requesting him to courier it to Lucknow. The bag itself was small, possibly made of animal skin. It would have to be packed securely before being handed over. He would then phone Fatima, and ask her to scatter the contents near their living quarters. With these troubled thoughts, Yusuf fell into a restless sleep, dreaming of sacrifices, pale-faced menacing figures who were half human and half animal, and for the first time, he imagined that even in his sleep, there was a presence standing beside his bed, observing him closely, if not menacingly.

The next day, Yusuf, using all his resources, could finally succeed in identifying someone who would be visiting Almora town for petty local purchases for the office. He asked his driver to proceed to the outpost, and hand over the now securely packed package to the office staff member, who had assured him that he would do the necessary job - it was a very minor one anyhow. The latter would also approach the most efficient and networked courier agency, if the courier charges were not the problem. Yusuf agreed that money was not the issue at all. In any case, the package was promptly delivered to Fatima, within four days; Yusuf had already instructed her telephonically on how to go about using it. His directions had left Fatima astonished. But she could sense the urgency in his voice and agreed to follow his instructions. Instead of scattering it in the wind (she could not understand the four directions aspect), she decided to scatter a tiny bit in each of the rooms which they had occupied, ignoring the one kept locked up. The kitchen and verandah would also get a tiny bit and be blessed, so Fatima reasoned. After cleaning her limbs, and donning fresh clothes, she did as directed, with Tahira looking on with innocent eyes. Fatima did not feel like sharing this action or discussing it with her in-laws next door. Somehow, she felt that they would regard her as an eccentric.

That night, Tahira sleeping next to Fatima on the bed, woke up with a scream. She clutched at her mother and sobbed loudly, "Ammi Ammi.. *bachao*.. please save me. They are taking me away.. Ammi Ammi, please.. !" Tahira's eyes were tightly closed and tears rolled down her cheeks, as she struggled with an unseen power which seemed to send her body into convulsions. The terrified Fatima held her child tightly to her bosom, trying to sooth her and console her, while Tahira continued to struggle and jerk. After a long time, she calmed down and fell into a deep slumber. Fatima could not sleep anymore that night. She kept vigil over her sleeping daughter, who twitched and murmured in her sleep, but did not once open her eyes. The rest of the night passed in this manner, and Fatima could finally snatch few winks as dawn was breaking. It was the first night of horror for them; more were yet to come.

During the day, Tahira was her usual cheerful self. She did not seem to remember anything from the previous night, and Fatima did not think it would be prudent to probe in this direction. Maybe it was just a bad dream. But in the back of her mind, her action of scattering some ashes, possibly having some magical powers, could have been a reason. Maybe her attempt to "purify" the place had actually aggravated and annoyed the entities lying in slumber. It was all very mysterious, but people, including children did have nightmares, did they not? Fatima was soon busy with her household chores. She also reasoned that it was high time that Tahira ought to be in school, so she could give vent to her excessive energies, instead of being cooped up in her playroom day and night. On her part, soon after breakfast, Tahira rushed off to her den. She hardly interacted with her cousins anymore, who now regarded her as a bit of a crank.

As Tahira assembled her toy train on its tracks, checking the tracks and other fittings, before starting its run, the child was suddenly aware of her unseen "friend" who was watching her keenly. Tahira glanced behind her shoulder, then seeing nothing, turned her attention once more to the elaborate toy train set, which was equipped with a rather long and winding track, working signals, tiny stations, bridges, figures of people, grazing animals and a tunnel. The train started its run, chugging slowly at first and then gathering speed. The console was in Tahira's hands, but as the train engine and its bogies, six in number, sped along, somehow the child lost control of the engine's movement. The train ran fast, then faster, not stopping at any of the stations and started to rush forward with terrifying speed, threatening to topple over at any second. The console was non-functional and in addition to the train's scary movement, the child could now feel that the presence in her room, her mysterious "friend" was no longer friendly. It was watching the goings-on with a malice which terrified the innocent child.

The toy train, in its mad rush, did not topple, but continued its uncontrolled journey, although sparks now flew from its electric components. Tahira continued to watch all this with horrified eyes, the console held uselessly in her hands; for the first time, she could sense not one but *two* invisible presences observing her malevolently, their gaze drilling into her back. Somehow, *they* wanted this charade of the toy train to end and the child to leave the room. The child was now an interloper, a nuisance, because the room belonged to *them* and *they* wanted privacy. And *they* would punish anyone who went against *their* wishes. All these negative feelings swamped the sensitive child's psyche and unable to bear the mental strain any longer, Tahira yelled loudly and rushed out her room. She continued to scream as her mother and aunts ran to embrace her and console her in whatever way possible. "Ammi!! Khala!! Save me. *Mujhe bachao*. They will kill me!!" screamed Tahira and collapsed in a faint.

After Tahira had been revived, and lay weeping on the bed, Fatima ventured to the playroom to try and understand what had actually happened. Were there intruders in the room, who had frightened her child? But how was that possible? Inside the room, Fatima saw that the toy train had toppled over; in places it had caught fire. The tracks and other fittings had become disjointed and lay strewn across the floor. Other than that, there was no sign of any intruder, human or otherwise. As an adult, Fatima did not possess that ESP which could have warned her that two malevolent beings, which did not belong to this material world, were still very much present in the room, observing her balefully. She hurriedly gathered the scattered parts of the toy, stuffing them in the box, and left the room, oblivious that she too had a close shave with something that she had inadvertently aroused, through her action of scattering ashes in the premises. Ashes over which certain incantations had been read, ashes which had the power to energise and provoke beings from the netherworld, which would then act as per their nature. A gentle personality would be helpful and benign; a spiteful being would be hostile and destructive.

Yusuf was unable to clearly understand Fatima's babble, as she tried to express herself incoherently over the phone, that too over a disturbed line. However, he immediately understood that something was seriously wrong and that he would have to reach Lucknow without further ado. But considering the route and official formalities, reaching home would take at least 24 hours if not less, including an overnight journey by train. While he made preparations to leave immediately, he also sounded his cousins staying in the premises; the latter promised all help and support. In fact, after that incident, they had not left Tahira's side for a moment,. A doctor had been summoned, who pronounced that the child had experienced some sort of mental trauma, but it was not usual for precocious children, who invariably had a lot of imagination and lived in a world of fantasy. He prescribed a mild sedative and Tahira was soon fast asleep, tucked up in her mother's bed.

For the rest of the extended family, excepting Fatima, the developments were not very surprising. They were vaguely aware of the history of the premises and the evil influence it harboured, especially the east wing. In fact, it was just a matter of time before something very unpleasant occurred. And it now seemed that Fatima had inadvertently precipitated the crisis through her actions. Whatever had started was expected. The house had been disturbed for over a century now, with no respite. Ill-luck seemed to follow its occupants, even after they had vacated it, and moved out of the city. Shoeb and Akhtar had continued to live in the west wing, simply because there was no other option; their combined incomes were too meagre and living in separate establishments, away from *Firaq Manzil*, was an impossibility. Also, the west wing appeared to be less accursed; disturbances were rare. In contrast, the east wing, where Yusuf had now settled his family, was prone to psychic disturbances, some frightening, others subtle. But a constant undercurrent of tension always seemed to be lurking there. The presence of the personal *Imambara* in the premises, the obsequies observed during *Muharram* and the occasional visits by *maulanas* or holy men did not appear to deter the supernatural activity present in the east wing. Shoeb remembered what his father (Yusuf's paternal uncle) had told him about the horrifying occurrences which he had faced several decades ago, forcing him to abandon his inheritance and migrate to Rampur. Apparently Yusuf's father had also died in a freak accident, his clothes catching fire without any reason, in the very room that was now the playroom of Tahira.

The next morning saw Yusuf hurriedly arriving at *Firaq Manzil*, much to the relief of his family. Tahira was delighted, hugging her father tightly, her frightening experience all but forgotten. Fatima was pale-faced as she greeted her husband, and the two sat down for breakfast. Somehow, the previous day's incident seemed trivial, when narrated in broad daylight, with a warm breeze blowing in the courtyard, and birds chirping, indicating an early summer. Tahira, fully recovered and overjoyed at seeing her father, skipped to her playroom and looked around. Her toy train set was in shambles - it seemed beyond repair. Undeterred, she settled down on the carpet, bringing out her impressive collection of Barbie dolls and their elaborate sets. Time flew by, with Tahira happily cooing, completely immersed in her make-believe world of dolls. She arranged and re-arranged their clothes, kitchen accessories and sports kits. Life was fun once again.

In the verandah outside, Yusuf and Fatima continued to be deep in conversation, discussing the present situation and future course of action. Chander's ominous warning continued to haunt Yusuf - he was unable to accept Tahira's scare of the previous day as something routine. Something ominous was active in the premises - that he was sure of, but he could not pinpoint what it was. He had heard tales of this house from his father and uncle; he was also convinced that something malefic, something sinister, had been stalking his family for almost a century now. But he was unable to make up his mind, make a decision and move. He had invested his meagre savings in refurbishing the dilapidated east wing; he could not take his wife and child back to the wilderness, where he was currently posted. So what was to be done? Fatima's wane face dampened his spirits and depressed him. Unable to come to any conclusion, he looked around but could not see Tahira around. The child had now been on her own for over two hours in her den. Yusuf decided to shake himself clear of morbid thoughts and join his daughter in a playful mood. He arose, and walked to the playroom, intending to greet his daughter with a hug and a kiss. But what he saw inside the room stunned him and set his heart pounding. Tahira lay on the floor, seemingly unconscious. Her clothes were half burnt, and so were her dolls, which were scattered across the floor in different directions. However, there was no smell of burning anywhere. What petrified Yusuf and brought him in cold sweat was the expression on the face of the comatose child. It was obvious that she had encountered something so hideous, seen something so dreadful, that losing consciousness had been her body's defence mechanism, rather than losing sanity.

III

1920

The Lucknow Pact of 1916 had re-united the Hindu and Muslim communities, paving the way for Gandhiji's Non-Cooperation Movement of 1920. The freedom movement gained momentum, although Sir Harcourt Butler, then Governor of the United Provinces, known for his inclusive approach, did his best to keep a watchful eye on the various communities then living in Lucknow, including his own compatriots. The Indians were full of resentment against their white "masters", with the latter doing nothing to assuage the feelings of the native population; in fact, their attitude towards the local populace was full of contempt and condescension. A time bomb was slowly ticking away, similar to the one which had exploded nearly sixty years ago, as India's First War of Independence. The Europeans or *firangis* generally avoided the old city, confining themselves to the Civil Lines or *Hazratganj* and of course, inside the new Cantonment at *Dilkusha*. But maverick British military officers and civilians did move around clandestinely in the lanes and bylanes of old Lucknow, for a variety of reasons, none of them good. One such officer was Captain Reginald Archer, popularly known as "Reggie" among his friends, not that he had many friends. Reggie was tall, stoutly built, with moderately good looks, a pug nose and shifty, restless eyes, greyish-green in colour. His undesirable habits and sexual predilections annoyed even his fellow officers. This army officer had got into the habit of donning civilian clothes, and moving around among the native populace, which generally avoided or ignored him. During one of his wanderings, this time in a crowded lane, known for serving spicy barbecued food, in the *Chowk* area, he came across a girl, whose beauty and sensual figure were obvious, even though she wore a *hijab*. Although Lucknow had no dearth of female beauties, something stirred inside Reggie, which was not pure lust. He observed the girl from a distance, which he shortened by taking long strides towards her. The girl, whose name was Aatifa observed this *saheb* approaching and shyly lowered her eyes, preferring to clutch her package of *kebabs* and hurry back to her home, which was *Firaq Manzil*.

Reggie watched her disappear inside a doorway; little did he know that the modest entrance led to rather spacious premises inside - the house owner being Ashar Ahmed, a local, wealthy landlord and a staunch supporter of the *Khilafat* Movement. Aware of the atrocities that his ancestors had faced during and after the events of 1857, Ahmed hated the colonial rulers with a vengeance. His only daughter, Aatifa, nubile, yet innocent, was not aware of her family's history. She was only mindful that a *gora* Saheb had made eye contact with her and his pointed stare had made her heart flutter. On his part, Reggie retreated, discretion being the better part of valour. But he had become restless now. His encounters with shady locals, including women of loose virtue had left him jaded. He suddenly had this desire of knowing this unknown girl better, on an intimate, personal level - knowing fully well that it would be an uphill task, that too fraught with danger.

Reggie returned to the cantonment, his mind in a whirl. He made a mental note of approaching his local contacts the very next day, after his regimental parade and other routine duties were over. He was aware of some Indian *sepoys* in his own regiment, who could be enticed into becoming informants. One such *sepoy*, Rafiq, already in trouble with his superiors, due to his outspoken political views, would be the best bet. This maverick *sepoy* could perhaps be assured of immunity against any official action against him, on the condition that he would delve into the antecedents of this nameless girl, who lived behind a modest gate, in the old city.

A month passed, with Rafiq agreeing to his Saheb's wishes and spreading his network far and wide, ultimately striking gold. One evening, greeting Reggie with a sloppy salute, which was more of a *salaam,* he spoke gleefully, "Saheb, I have done your work. You must give me big reward."

Reggie, who was lounging in the verandah of his official army bungalow, a glass of whiskey in his hand, stared at Rafiq with unfocussed eyes.

"Chup karo, bakwas band karo!!" he snapped, "Kaam ki baat bolo!!"

Undeterred, Rafiq went on to relate how Ashar Ahmed was in trouble as he did not have the necessary papers to prove his ownership and inheritance of the sprawling ancestral property where he resided. If Reggie could put in a good word with the local British magistrate, who would then allow Ashar to prepare and submit papers afresh as proof of his inheritance, Ashar's problems would be solved to a great extent. In due course of time, things did materialise as Rafiq had predicted. Although the *sepoy* did not get any benefit out of his cloak-and-dagger operations (in fact, he was marched out of Lucknow to Agra cantonment, at the instance of Reggie's superior, a red faced Irishman named Col. MacClery), Reggie and Ashar Ahmed quickly became close friends. And this paved the way for Reggie's visits to *Firaq Manzil*, which sent Aatifa's heart fluttering, as she observed this dashing British officer in full army regalia, relaxing in the *dewan khana* of *Firaq Manzil*. Admiration soon changed to mutual infatuation, and both searched for a way to meet alone, far from the prying eyes of the family and community.

Reggie and Aatifa did not have to wait long. During one of his sudden visits to *Firaq Manzil*, that too in the daytime on an off-day, Ashar invited him to stay back for lunch. Excusing himself for a moment, Ashar hurried out to the nearby market for buying provisions, instructing his daughter to serve drinking water to their honoured guest. As Reggie lounged on an easy chair in the *dewan khana*, Aatifa entered the room, the anklets on her feet tinkling sweetly. Her heart fluttered wildly in her breast and her hands trembled, as she held out a tray containing *sherbet* and sweetmeats. Reggie gently took the tray from her and kept it on the table. While Aatifa stood before him with downcast eyes, he took both her warm, delicate hands in his own, and drew her close. Passion welled up in their young hearts, as Reggie pulled her closer, making her sit on his lap. She threw her arms around his neck, holding him tightly, while he smothered her beautiful face with passionate kisses. Their lips met, as Reggie groped her and fondled her supple breasts under her dress. Time stood still for both, as they explored each other frantically, oblivious of the dangers they faced. That moment was pure magic, but it would be torn asunder in a matter of minutes.

His purchases over, Ashar entered the *dewan khana* jauntily, and was momentarily stunned at what he saw. He seemed to freeze with shock, his blood congealing, then his anger and old resentment for the *gora log*, the *firangis* swamped his senses. The thought that his own daughter could be equally guilty for this indiscretion did not cross his mind, which had seemingly blanked out.

"*Lā hawla walā quwwat*," growled Ashar in a choked voice, and snatching a decorative sword adorning the wall, he rushed at the couple, intending to make short work of this infidel. On hearing her father's angry mutter, Aatifa's eyes jerked open and in a split second, as a reflexive action, she pushed Reggie sideways, away from her. The sword swerved, and missing Reggie's unprotected back, it entered her throat. The rush of the weapon was so forceful, and its blade so keen, that it all but sliced her head off. As she fell on the floor, blood spouting from her severed throat in great spurts, Reggie looked at his dying lover with horrified eyes, oblivious of the fact that the next swing of the sword would take his life, as it plunged into his back, severing his heart into two.

Maddened by grief, anger and self-mortification, Ashar continued to hack at the dying British officer with the sword, severing his limbs and gouging out the eyes, which had cast their sinful look on Aatifa. As the dying lovers lay on the floor, life slowly ebbing out, their blood intermixing in death, their spirits, now released from their bodies, observed their own mutilated mortal remains on the blood-spattered floor. The anguish of their unrequited love, the uncontrolled momentary passion both had experienced, and the terrible rage at being deprived of the pleasures of flesh, unleashed their curse on Ashar, his family, the house where they lived and the room where the massacre had taken place. *Firaq Manzil* was doomed from that moment onwards. It would never find peace again.

As sanity returned to Ashar and he struggled to gain control over his berserk mind, he looked at his own doing with horrified eyes. He had murdered his own daughter, whom he adored, and he had killed and mutilated a serving British army officer. The servants of the house, who had rushed to the scene of the mayhem, held his arms tightly, as he continued to rant and rave, ultimately collapsing, his body heaving with sobs, as he grieved for his daughter and the terrible tragedy that he had invited upon himself. He had no misgivings about what would happen now. Retribution would be swift - not only would he be arrested and hanged, it was entirely possible that his neighbours and his community too would face British wrath. His thoughts now under control, and under the counsel of his servants, it was decided to dig a shallow grave in a corner of the room where the tragedy had occurred. It would serve as a burial place for the unfortunate Aatifa. With the severed head lolling to one side, there was no way that she could be given a proper funeral and interred in a graveyard, as per the tenets of Islam. The hacked body of Reggie was carried to a corner behind the east wing of the property and set on fire with kerosene, to prevent identification. Ashar hoped that Reggie would not have confided to anyone about his clandestine visit to the old quarter of the city - an activity which was frowned upon by the colonial administration. But burning a human body, with limited resources, is not an easy job. Realising the futility of this exercise, it was decided to dump Reggie's partially burnt body into the unused well, and board it up. The room of the tragedy was cleaned, all traces of blood and struggle removed, and incense sticks burnt over the freshly dug grave of the unfortunate Aatifa. The floor stones were re-affixed over the spot; soon it would be impossible to identify that one corner of the room had been dug up, into which the mortal remains of a murdered young girl had been interred. The room was closed and locked. The gruesome events of the day came to close and the family servants were sworn to secrecy.

Aatifa had lost her mother at a very young age. It was Ashar who had raised her with all the love and affection that a single parent could provide. That night, Ashar could not sleep. He tossed and turned, trying to blank out his mind from re-living the horrors of the day. And as he drifted into an uneasy slumber, he thought that he could see his dead wife standing at the foot of his bed. She was as beautiful as ever, but her eyes were streaked with tears. The vision slowly faded and he could feel his own body wracked with sobs. But wait.. who was running on the verandah of the inner courtyard of this rambling house at this hour? From the pitter-patter, it appeared to be a young child. Someone giggled.. a sound he could immediately recognise as that of Aatifa, when she had been a child. But no.. Aatifa was not a child anymore, was she? She had grown up to become a beautiful young woman. And now Aatifa was dead; brutally killed. Her head severed from her body. She could not even have the *Salat al-Janazah* prayers recited for her after her death, such was her unfortunate fate - forced as she was to lie under paving stones, in an unmarked grave, inside a room of her own house.

Ashar continued to doze fitfully, his mind on the verge on insanity. Sometime during the night, he felt something glowering in the dark. He could sense two baleful eyes looking malevolently at him, even though his own eyelids were closed. The staring eyes were grey-green.. like the dead Reggie's eyes.. but Reggie was not there. Something was on fire. His bed, his own body. His bedclothes. There was fire everywhere. But it did not hurt. Nothing could hurt him anymore. He was like one possessed by an *ifrit*, a demon, which now controlled his actions and senses and had him at its mercy.

IV

2020

A forest rest house, five kilometres away from Almora town, was to be the temporary home for Yusuf and his family. They had hurriedly left *Firaq Manzil* after the tragedy and had reached Almora after a tedious journey by train and road. Tahira had recovered from her shock, but appeared to be dull and listless after that incident. Yusuf and Fatima had unanimously decided that the ancestral house was not safe for them, whatever might be the reason. If Tahira had to stay away from her husband in any case, she could settle in Haldwani or Almora or even Dehra. But Lucknow was now out of question. Yusuf's cousins had agreed to dispatch his belongings as soon as some sort of permanent establishment had been finalised for Fatima and Tahira, after which Yusuf would re-join at Rikiyasain, his current place of posting. In the meantime, Yusuf had made up his mind to be constantly beside his family and assure them that the danger was gone.

The typical cottage-style rest house was cosy and sunny. Surrounded by tall trees and lush greenery, husband and wife felt secure and happy after a long hiatus. The full time cook-cum-*chowkidar* was a sturdy, affable fellow, who could rustle up simple meals without much ado, and also look after their day-to-day comforts. The young parents felt reassured and convinced that Tahira would soon recover from her trauma and become her cheerful self once more. The child, however, preferred to stay indoors, staring blankly in front of her. No longer playful or chirpy, she seemed to have acquired a new personality altogether.

One evening saw Yusuf and Fatima relaxing in the living room of the rest house. Tahira was nowhere to be seen. It was dark and forbidding outside, with clouds scudding across an overcast sky - signalling a sudden thunderstorm so characteristic of the hills. Desiring to have their daughter sit with them in the cosy confines of the living room, the young parents arose and entered their bedroom. Inside, they found Tahira sitting on a low chair; her eyes were blank, staring into space as she muttered to herself. She seemed to be talking unintelligibly to someone in low tones. This ghastly sight sent a shiver up the spines of husband and wife. Realising that Tahira had not yet recovered from her ordeal, Fatima rushed forward, lifting the child and hugging her to her breast. Tahira did not seem to recognise her mother; she remained limp like a lifeless doll.

Behind them, a glass of water kept on the corner table slowly moved to the edge on its own and toppled over, splashing its contents on the floor.

SUGGESTED READINGS

Abdul Ali, AFM, *The Last Will and Testament of Bahu Begum* (1926), N. Mukherjee, Art Press, Calcutta.

Abidi, HA, "Begum Hazrat Mahal", *Naya Daur*, No. 5 (1966) pp. 45 – 48.

Abu, TKM, *Tafzihul Ghafilin* [The Disgrace of The Negligent], translated from Farsi by William Hoey, *History of Asafud Daulah, Nawab Wazir of Oudh*, Government Press, Allahabad (Reprint, Pustak Kendra, Lucknow, 1971).

Ahmad, EU, *Formation and End of a Mughal Provincial Civilization: A Socio-Economic and Cultural History of Awadh* (2008), Thesis for Ph.D, Aligarh Muslim University, Aligarh.

Ahmad, Muhammad Taqi (translation), *Tarikh Badshah Begam* (1938), The Indian Press Ltd., Allahabad.

Anonymous (*ed.*), *Gazetteer of the Province of Oudh, Vol. II - H - M* (1877), Allahabad.

Anonymous (*ed.*), *Unao: A Gazetteer, being Vol, XXXVIII of the District Gazetteers of the United Provinces of Agra and Oudh* (1903), Allahabad.

Anonymous (*ed.*), *Papers Relating to The Affairs of Oude 1808, 1834, 1853, 1856*, Calcutta.

Anonymous, *The Story of The Indian Mutiny 1857 - 58* (1898), WP Nimmo, Hay & Mitchell, Edinburgh.

Basu, Purnendu, *Oudh and the East India Company: 1785-1801* (1943), Maxwell Company, Lucknow.

Bird, RW, *The Spoliation of Oudh* (1857), Nassau Steam Press, Charing Cross, London, UK.

Blunt, EAH, *Christian Tombs and Tablets of Historical Interest in the United Provinces of Agra and Oudh* (1911), Govt. Press, Allahabad.

Brock, William, *A Biographical Sketch of Sir Henry Havelock, KCB* (1858), Bernhard Tauchnitz, Leipzig.

Brunton, Bruce, "The East India Company: Agent of Empire in the Early Modern Capitalist India", *Social Education*, Vol. 77(2) (2013) pp. 78 - 81.

Buckland, CE, *Dictionary of Indian Biography* (1906), Swan Sonnenschein, London.

Compton, Herbert, *A Particular Account of the European Military Adventurers of Hindustan From 1784 to 1803* (1892), T Fisher Unwin, London.

Deloche, Jean, and Dutta-Baruah, Caroline (translation and commentary), *Adventures of Jean-Baptiste Chevaliar in Eastern India: 1752 - 1765* (2008), LBS Publications, Guwahati.

Dodd, George, *The History of The Indian Revolt, 1856-7-8* (1859), W&R Chambers, London.

Dodwell, Henry, *Dupleix and Clive: The Beginning of Empire* (1920), Methuen, London.

Edwardes, Michael, *Battles of the Indian Mutiny* (1963), BT Batsford, London.

Edwardes, Michael, *The Orchid House: Splendours and Miseries of The Kingdom of Oudh,* 1827 - 1857 (1960), Ebenezer & Son, London.

Fitchett, WH, *The Tale of The Great Mutiny* (1902), Smith, Elder & Co., London.

Forbes-Mitchell, William, *Reminiscences of the Great Mutiny 1857- 59* (1893 / 1910), Macmillan, London.

Forrest, GW (*ed.*), *Selections from the Letters, Dispatches and Other State Papers Preserved by The Military Department of The Government of India: 1857 – 58,* Vol. I (1893) and Vol. II (1902), Military Department Press, Calcutta.

Fremont-Barnes, G, *Essential Histories, The Indian Mutiny 1857 - 58* (2007), Osprey Publishing, Oxford.

Fuerst, IRM, *Indian Muslim Minorities and the 1857 Rebellion. Religion, Rebels, and Jihad* (2017), IB Tauris, London.

Fuhrer, A, *The Monumental Antiquities and Inscriptions of the North-West Provinces and Oudh* (1891), Archaeological Survey of India, Allahabad.

Gole, Susan, *Maps of Mughal India: Drawn by Jean-Baptiste-Joseph Gentil, Agent for the French government to the Court of Shuja-ud-Daula at Faizabad, in 1770* (1988), Manohar, Delhi.

Gordon-Alexander, W, *Recollections of A Highland Subaltern* (1898), Edward Arnold, London.

Grey, Charles, *European Adventurers of Northern India 1785 - 1849* (1929), Government Printing Press, Lahore.

Gubbins, Martin R, *An Account of the Mutinies in Oudh and the Siege of the Lucknow Residency* (1858), Richard Bentley, London, UK.

Hale, WP, *The Oude Question* (1857), Smith & Co., London.

Harcourt, ES and Hussain, Fakhir (translation), *Lucknow: The Last Phase of an Oriental Culture by Abdul Halim Sharar* (1989), Oxford University Press, New Delhi.

Headley, JT, *The Life of General H. Havelock, KCB* (1861), Charles Scribner, New York.

Hibbert, Christopher, *The Great Mutiny India 1857* (1978), The Viking Press, New York.

Hill, SC, *The Life of Claud Martin* (1901), Thacker, Spink & Co, Calcutta.

Hussain, MS, *Cartoons from the Oudh Punch* (1881), The Oudh Punch Press, Lucknow.

Hutchinson, George, *Narrative of The Mutinies in Oude* (1859), Cranenburgh Military Orphan Press, Calcutta.

Irvine, William, *Later Mughals Vol II: 1719 – 1739* (1922), MC Sarkar & Sons, Calcutta.

Irwin, HC, *The Garden of India or Chapters on Oudh History and Affairs* (1880), WH Allen, London.

Ivermee, Robert, *Hooghly: The Global History of A River* (2020), Hurst & Co, London.

Jafri, SZH (*ed.*), *Delhi and Awadh During 1857, Studies, Images and Documents* (2020), Gyan Publishing House, New Delhi.

Keene, HG, *Hindustan Under Free Lances* (1907), Brown & Langham, London.

Khan, IG, "The Awadh Scientific Renaissance and The Role of The French", *Indian Journal of History of Science*, 38(3) (2003) pp. 273 - 301.

Kumari, Rashmi, *Maulavi Ahmad Ullah Shah and Great Revolt of 1857* (2016) (translated by Srivastava, M), National Book Trust, New Delhi.

La Touche, THD, *The Journals of Major James Rennell* (1910), Baptist Mission Press, Calcutta.

Lacoste, Anne, *Felice Beato, The Eastern Road* (2010), Paul Getty Museum, Los Angeles.

Lafont, Jean-Marie, *Indika: Essays in Indo-French Relations 1630 - 1976* (2000), Manohar, Delhi.

Lauriston, Jean Law, *A Memoir of the Mughal Empire: Events of 1757 - 1761* (2014) (translated by Cheema, GS), Manohar, Delhi.

Laws, RA, *Lucknow Society and Politics* (1979), Thesis for Ph.D, University of North South Wales, Sydney.

Leckey, Edward, *Fictions Connected With The Indian Outbreak of 1857 Exposed* (1859), Chesson & Woodhall, Bombay.

Lovett, AC and MacMunn, GF, *The Armies of India* (1911), Adam & Charles Black, London.

Low, CR, *Major General Sir Frederick S Roberts, A Memoir* (1883), WH Allen, London.

Mackenzie, ARD, *Mutiny Memoirs being the Personal Reminiscences of the Great Sepoy Revolt of 1857* (1891), Pioneer Press, Allahabad.

MacPhee, G and Poddar, P (*eds.*), *Empire and After: Englishness in Postcolonial Perspective* (2007), Berghahn, New York.

Majumdar, RC, *The Sepoy Mutiny and The Revolt of 1857* (1963), Firma KL Mukhopadhyay, Calcutta.

Malleson, GB, *History of The French in India* (1909), John Grant, Edinburgh.

Malleson, GB (*ed.*), *Kaye's and Malleson's History of the Indian Mutiny of 1857 - 58* (1889), WH Allen, London.

Malleson, GB, *The Indian Mutiny of 1857* (1891), Seeley & Co. Ltd., London.

Marshman, JC, *Memoirs of Major General Sir Henry Havelock, KCB* (1881), Longman, Green & Co, London.

Maude, FC, *Memories of The Mutiny* Vol. II (1894), Remington and Co, London.

Mecham, CH, *Sketches and Incidents of the Siege of Lucknow* (1858), Day & Son, London.

Mehta, Asoka, *1857 The Great Rebellion* (1946), Hind Kitabs Ltd., Bombay.

Mevissen, GJR and Banerji, Arundhati (*eds*), *Prajñādhara* (2009), Kaveri Books, New Delhi.

Mukherjee, Rudrangshu, *Awadh in Revolt: 1857 – 1858* (2001), Permanent Black, Delhi.

Nagar, Amritlal, *Gathering The Ashes* (2014) (translated by Pande, M), Harper Perennial, New Delhi.

Outram, James, Lieut. *General Sir James Outram's Campaign in India, 1857 - 1858* (1860), Smith, Elder & Co., London.

Pandey, US, *European Adventurers in North India* (2019), Routledge, New Delhi.

Perkins, CR, "From the Mehfil to the printed word: Public Debate and Discourse in late Colonial India", *The Economic and Social History Review*, 50(1) (2013), pp. 47-76.

Praed, Winthrop (*ed.*), *Papers Relative To The Succession To The Throne of Oude* (1838), Calcutta.

Qureshi, HA, *The Mughals, The English & The Rulers of Awadh from 1722 AD to 1856 AD. A Kaleidoscopic Study* (2003), New Royal Book Company, Lucknow.

Rees, Ruutz LW, *Personal Narrative of the Siege of Lucknow* (1858), Longman, London.

Rizvi, SAA and Bhargava, ML (*eds.*), *Freedom Struggle in Uttar Pradesh Vol II, Awadh: 1857-59* (1958), Publications Bureau, Prayag.

Rizvi, SNR and Jafri, SZH (*eds.*), *The Great Uprising of 1857: Commentaries, Studies and Documents* (2009), Anamika Publishers, New Delhi.

Roberts, Frederick, *Forty One Years in India: From Subaltern to Commander-in-Chief* (1901) Macmillan, London.

Roy, Malini, *Idiosyncrasies in the Late Mughal Painting Tradition, The Artist Mihr Chand, son of Ganga Ram* (2009), Thesis for Ph.D, SOAS, University of London, London.

Sarkar, PC, *Abode of Fairies - Lucknow's Parikhana* (2022), Kalpaz, New Delhi.

Sarkar, PC, *Lucknow - Ode To A City* (2021), Kalpaz, New Delhi.

Sarkar, PC, *Lucknow: Buildings, Begums and The British* (2015), Kalpaz, New Delhi.

Savarkar, V, The *Indian War of Independence 1857* (1909), Abhishek Publications, Chandigarh.

Saxena, RB, *A History of Urdu Literature* (1927), Ram Narain Lal, Allahahad.

Sedgwick, FR, *The Indian Mutiny of 1857 - A Sketch of the Principal Military Events* (1909), Forster Groom, London.

Sen SP, *The French in India: 1763 -1816* (1958), FKL Mukhopadhyay, Calcutta.

Sen, SN, *Eighteen Fifty-Seven* (1957), Publications Division, Govt. of India, New Delhi.

Sleeman, William H., *A Journey Through the Kingdom of Oudh in 1849 – 1850*, Vols 1 & 2 (1858), Richard Bentley, London, UK.

Srivastava, AL, *Shuja-ud-Daulah Vol I: 1754 – 1765* (1961), SL Agarwala, Agra.

Srivastava, AL, *Shuja-ud-Daulah Vol II: 1765 – 1775* (1945), Minerva, Lahore.

Srivastava, AL, *The First Two Nawabs of Awadh* (1954), SL Agarwala, Agra.

Stark, U, "Politics, Public Issues and Promotion of Urdu Literature: Avadh Akhbar, the First Urdu Daily in Northern India", *Annual of Urdu Studies*, 8 (2003), pp. 66 - 94.

Stark, U, *An Empire of Books* (2007), Permanent Black, Ranikhet.

Sutton, Thomas, *The Daniells: Artists and Travellers* (1954), Bodley Head, London.

Taban, FA, "The Coming of the Revolt in Awadh: The Evidence of Urdu Newspapers", *Social Scientist*, 26 (1998), pp. 1 - 16.

Thackeray, ET, *Two Indian Campaigns in 1857 - 58* (1896), WJ Mackay, Chatham.

Tieffenthaler, Joseph, *Description Historique et Gèographique De L'Inde, Tome 1* (1786), Rennel, Berlin.

Tribunus, "Some Notices of General Claud Martin", *Bengal Past & Present*, Vol. II (Part II) (1908), pp. 280 - 287.

White, W, *Mirza Kaiwan Jah or the Dethroned King of Oude in Chains!!*(1838), William Strange, London.

White, W, *The Prince of Oude, or The Claim of the Nawaub Ekbal-Ood-Dowlah Bahadur To The Throne of Awadh* (1838), William Strange, London.

Wood, Evelyn, *The Revolt in Hindustan* (1908), Methuen, London.

Wylly, HC, *A Life of Lieutenant-General Sir Eyre Coote, KB* (1922), Clarendon, Oxford.

Index

C

G

H

M

N

O

Y

Z